CHOCOLATE
GALORE

CHOCOLATE
GALORE

CAROLINE BARTY

spruce

An Hachette Livre UK Company

First published in Great Britain in 2008
by Spruce, a division of
Octopus Publishing Group Ltd
2–4 Heron Quays, London E14 4JP
www.octopusbooks.co.uk

Photography: Ian Garlick
Food Styling: Eliza Baird
Page Layout: Balley Design Associates

ISBN 13: 978-1-84601-148-1

A CIP catalogue record of this book is
available from the British Library.

Printed and bound in China

10 9 8 7 6 5 4 3 2 1

CONTENTS

INTRODUCTION

It is the cacao tree, indigenous to the regions of Central and South America, which provides us with the raw material for making chocolate. The cacao seed or bean is roasted, fermented, dried and ground to leave cacao (or cocoa) powder.

★ ORIGINS ★

It is generally thought that the Mayans, living in the Yucatán and Guatemala in the first millennia AD, were the first people to cultivate and use the cacao tree. However, evidence suggests that the Mayans learnt their knowledge from an earlier Olmec culture, around 1500–400 BC. Mayan traders would have introduced the cacao bean to the Aztecs and it soon became of huge importance in both cultures. Warriors and noblemen were buried with vessels for drinking chocolate and chocolate was offered to the gods as ceremonial gifts.

Christopher Columbus was known to have brought back some cocoa beans to the Spanish court but it wasn't until later when Cortés returned from the New World that the popularity of the cocoa bean really took off. So a commodity was born that generated great power and wealth. The Spanish were credited with giving chocolate its name – an amalgam of the Mayan 'chocol', meaning hot, and the Aztec 'atl', meaning water.

By the 1600s chocolate was known throughout Europe although it seems to have been its mythical medicinal qualities that first appealed to people. Chocolate does in fact contain a small amount of phenylethylamine, which is a chemical that produces a feeling of a natural 'high'. It was the arrival of sugar from America that really cemented the popularity of chocolate. Drinking sweetened chocolate became a popular pastime although still only for the wealthy.

★ THE CHOCOLATE BAR ★

The idea of mixing cocoa butter, the by-product of making cocoa powder, with the powder itself came about in the early 1800s. A smooth paste, solid when cold, was created that gave us the early form of what we know as the chocolate bar. It was the Swiss who refined the art of chocolate making by inventing the process known as conching. The chocolate is constantly moved at a temperature of between 55–85°C thus exposing it to air, which improves its flavour and extracts more fat from the cocoa. The Swiss also developed the milk chocolate bar by adding dried milk to the chocolate-making process. White chocolate is not strictly chocolate as it does not contain cocoa mass but is a blend of cocoa butter, sugar and milk solids.

★ LIMITLESS FLAVOURS ★

As the flavour of chocolate improved so chefs were inspired to create wonderful confections. Nuts, fruit and flavourings were added, chocolate was moulded into different shapes and filled with soft fondant or liqueurs. There is always a heated debate as to which country makes the finest chocolates. Belgium, Switzerland or France all have a good case to put forward but ultimately it comes down to personal tastes. Some diehard chocoholics would not touch a bitter square of plain chocolate yet others see milk chocolate as an inferior product, barely worthy of being called chocolate at all. Whatever your view there is no disputing that chocolate is one of life's great pleasures.

COOKING WITH CHOCOLATE

As with all things, the better the quality the better the taste and chocolate is no exception.

Nowadays the range of superior-quality chocolate available is enormous. There is absolutely no excuse to buy what they call chocolate-flavour cake covering. Avoid it at all costs. Professional confectioners tend to use couverture chocolate. It has a high cocoa butter content and so melts easily and when set has a pleasing glossy finish. However it is only available in specialist shops so is not used in any of these recipes.

For the fullest flavour I recommend chocolate with at least 70% cocoa solids but in some recipes its intensity is overpowering and so a chocolate with 50% cocoa solids actually produces a more delicate flavour. If it is not obvious from the front, if you read the list of ingredients on the back of a bar of chocolate it will tell you the amount of cocoa solids present.

You will also find that chocolate with less cocoa solids will melt more easily and will be less likely to 'seize'. This is when the chocolate overheats and becomes stiff and grainy. It will also seize when any cold moisture comes into contact with it. This is why it is essential to let melted chocolate cool a little before incorporating it with anything else.

★ MELTING CHOCOLATE ★

I have to say I always use a microwave to melt chocolate but you have to bear in mind that microwave power varies greatly. Start off on high power but for 10–20 seconds at a time. This way you won't burn the chocolate and you will soon find how long your own microwave takes to melt the chocolate. In general it takes between 1 and 2 minutes to melt a bowl of chocolate but obviously the larger the quantity the longer it will take.

If you don't have a microwave you will need to fit a mixing bowl or pudding basin over the top of a saucepan with a small quantity of hot water in the bottom. This is then placed over a gentle heat until the chocolate melts. The most important thing is not to let the bowl come into contact with the water. Not only will the chocolate overheat, but the water sputters out from the sides and comes into contact with the chocolate, which then seizes. Some people with Agas swear by melting chocolate in a bowl in the bottom oven and the few times I have tried this it seems to work very well. In some cases you can melt chocolate over a direct heat but only when the chocolate is being melted with another liquid such as cream. Never melt chocolate on its own over a direct heat.

★ TEMPERING CHOCOLATE ★

Tempering is the name given to the process whereby chocolate is melted and worked to produce a chocolate with a glossy, even finish. If you want a professional finish to confectionery, especially when making moulded chocolate, you will need to temper the chocolate. However, it is tricky due to the precise temperatures required for heating and cooling and will take a bit of practice. The simplest method is to melt the chocolate then pour two-thirds onto a marble slab. With a palette knife work it backwards and forwards until it is just on the point of setting. Return it to the remaining third and remelt it. It can now be used for moulds and decorations.

CHOCOLATE DECORATIONS

You can buy all sorts of chocolate-based decorations in the supermarket these days, but the quality of chocolate varies greatly so have a go at making your own.

★ CHOCOLATE PIPING ★

The quickest and simplest way for fine chocolate piping is to get a greaseproof paper piping bag, fill with a little melted chocolate and snip a tiny bit off the end. Then you can write or drizzle the melted chocolate over the surface. When it is on the point of setting chocolate ganache (see page 154) can be piped using an ordinary piping bag and starred nozzle.

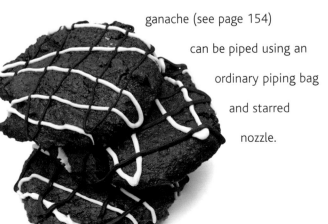

★ GRATING CHOCOLATE ★

The microplane graters do a good job at grating chocolate. Putting the chocolate in the refridgerator for 15 minutes will make it easier to grate. Try not to handle the chocolate as it will melt more quickly. Wrapping the end of the chocolate in foil will prevent the heat from your hands melting the chocolate.

★ QUICK CHOCOLATE CURLS ★

First make sure the chocolate is at room temperature. With a potato peeler, peel off little curls from the edge of the chocolate bar.

★ CHOCOLATE CARAQUE ★

Another name for big chocolate curls. Melt 120–150g chocolate and pour over a marble slab. Leave it to harden. It needs to be hard but not completely set. At a 45° angle to the surface draw the blade of a small sharp knife across the chocolate, away from the body. Turn the point of the knife a little as if you are about to trace a circle. The chocolate should form long curls. It is crucial to get the correct angle of the blade and also that the chocolate is at the right temperature. Too hot and the curls will collapse and too cold, i.e. set, and the chocolate will form shards rather than curls.

★ CHOCOLATE LEAVES ★

Firstly you will need the leaves of a non-toxic plant. Rose and bay leaves are best as they have well-defined veins. Wash the leaves and leave to dry completely. Melt the chocolate and paint the underside of the leaves with chocolate. Leave to harden and set, then carefully peel off the leaves.

BUYING & STORING CHOCOLATE

Always check the use by date on chocolate as some shops are less than scrupulous about their stock turnover. Plain chocolate tends to have a longer shelf life than milk chocolate, about one year compared to six months. Always keep chocolate in a cool, dry place. If it is very hot it can be kept in the refrigerator but it can become discoloured due to the difference in temperatures. This does not affect its flavour and it can be used in the normal way.

INGREDIENTS

Before cocoa was mixed with sugar to become chocolate it was used predominantly in savoury dishes. Most people have heard of turkey mole and chilli con carne, two well-known Mexican dishes, where a little chocolate is added to enhance and add a new dimension. Chapter Seven, New Ways with Chocolate, includes these two favourites and re-introduces chocolate and cocoa into a variety of other main course dishes. Here is a list of the most commonly used ingredients when baking sweet dishes using chocolate.

★ BUTTER ★

Try and use the butter that the recipe specifies. The flavour of salted butter can really spoil a dessert or confectionery as can cheap margarine.

★ COCOA POWDER ★

Cocoa powder is chocolate liquor that has had most of the cocoa butter removed and is dried into a very fine powder. Whatever you do don't confuse cocoa powder with drinking chocolate. Cocoa powder is unsweetened and should have no other additives. Dutch cocoa powder is the best as it is processed to reduce the acids that occur naturally in chocolate.

★ PLAIN CHOCOLATE ★

Most recipes will specify which plain chocolate to use, usually between 50 and 70% cocoa solids. Taste different brands to find your favourite as they can vary greatly.

★ COUVERTURE CHOCOLATE ★

Couverture chocolate is what professional chocolatiers use for their work. It has a high cocoa butter content that when melted, produces a runny chocolate that covers in an even, glossy finish.

EQUIPMENT

Apart from the obvious cake tins, muffin tins etc. there is not much specialist equipment needed for cooking with chocolate. However, a sugar thermometer is essential for a few of the recipes in the Chocolaterie chapter and is a great help for other recipes. Most good cookshops sell them. Another invaluable item in the kitchen is nonstick baking parchment. Even if you have non-stick bakeware it is best to base-line your tins. If you have a food processor with a balloon whisk and dough hook attachments all the better, but it is not a necessity. To incorporate as much air as possible into your baking it is best to have an electric hand-held whisk.

★ MILK CHOCOLATE ★

There is a huge difference between good and bad milk chocolate. Try and buy one of the expensive brands and you really will notice the difference, both in flavour and texture.

★ WHITE CHOCOLATE ★

As mentioned, white chocolate is not actually chocolate at all as it contains no cocoa solids. Cheap white chocolate can be tricky to melt and can seize very easily if it comes into contact with a liquid or even a utensil with a different temperature. I always warm a metal spoon under hot water for a minute and dry it really well before using it to stir melted white chocolate.

THE BAKERY

DOUBLE CHOC-CHIP COOKIES

These cookies are the ultimate chocolate experience – double the chocolate, double the taste!

MAKES 14 COOKIES

150g butter
150g caster sugar
1 egg, beaten
1–2 teaspoons vanilla extract
200g plain flour
1 teaspoon baking powder
50g good-quality plain chocolate, broken into pieces
50g good-quality white chocolate, broken into pieces

1. Preheat the oven to 180°C/gas mark 4. Lightly grease a baking sheet.

2. Beat together the butter and sugar until pale and fluffy. Beat in the egg and vanilla extract. Sift the flour and baking powder together and beat into the mixture. Add the chocolate and stir until mixed.

3. Place 5–6 rounded tablespoons of the cookie mixture onto the baking sheet at a time, leaving plenty of space between them as the cookies will almost double in size. Bake for 12–15 minutes until golden.

4. Leave to cool on the baking sheet for 2–3 minutes, then transfer to a wire rack to cool completely. Cookies can be stored in an airtight container for up to 1 week.

CHOCOLATE GRANOLA BARS

These bars are a sort of spongy flapjack. I like to use a nutty granola but you can use your favourite cereal as long as it is the crunchy variety rather than a muesli.

MAKES 10–12 BARS

120g unsalted butter,
   slightly softened
120g soft brown sugar
1 egg, beaten
120g plain flour
200g crunchy granola
100g plain chocolate
   (70% cocoa solids),
   finely chopped

1. Preheat the oven to 180°C/gas mark 4. Base-line a 22cm square cake tin with non-stick baking parchment.

2. Beat the butter and sugar until light and fluffy. Beat in the egg. Fold in the flour followed by the granola and chocolate.

3. Spoon into the prepared tin and level out the surface. Bake for 20–25 minutes until firm to the touch. Cool in the tin, then cut into bars.

WHITE CHOCOLATE & BUTTER PECAN COOKIES

These cookies freeze really well so if you make more than you need pop the cookies in a freezer bag and seal. Defrost at room temperature for one hour.

MAKES ABOUT 30 COOKIES

150g unsalted butter,
   slightly softened
120g soft brown sugar
150g caster sugar
2 eggs, beaten
2 teaspoons vanilla extract
300g plain flour
1 teaspoon baking powder
Pinch of salt
100g white chocolate morsels or
   finely chopped white chocolate
100g pecans, finely chopped

1. Preheat the oven to 180°C/gas mark 4.

2. Cream the butter and sugars together until light and fluffy. Beat in the eggs and vanilla extract. Stir in the remaining ingredients in order.

3. Take tablespoons of the dough and roll into balls. Place on a non-stick baking sheet about 5–6cm apart and press down slightly. Bake in batches for 10–15 minutes until they are turning golden around the edges.

4. Remove from the oven and leave to harden for a minute or two before placing on a wire rack to cool completely.

CHOCOLATE HAZELNUT & VANILLA WHIRLS

These attractive and flavoursome little cookies are surprisingly simple to make.

MAKES ABOUT 30 COOKIES

175g butter, plus extra
　for greasing
75g icing sugar
1 teaspoon vanilla extract
225g plain flour, sifted,
　plus extra for dusting
2 tablespoons chocolate
　and hazelnut spread
1 tablespoon unsweetened
　cocoa powder, sifted

1. Preheat the oven to 160°C/gas mark 3. Lightly grease a baking sheet.

2. Beat together the butter and sugar until pale and fluffy. Beat in the vanilla extract. Add the flour and work into the mixture to form a soft dough.

3. Divide the dough into two pieces and work the chocolate and hazelnut spread and cocoa powder into one half.

4. Roll each piece of dough on a lightly floured surface to form two rectangles about 15 x 20cm. If the dough is too soft to roll, chill wrapped in clingfilm for 10–15 minutes to firm slightly.

5. Place one piece of dough on top of the other and press together lightly. Trim the edges and roll up lengthways like a Swiss roll. Cover and chill for 30 minutes.

6. Cut the dough into 6mm slices and space well apart on the baking sheet. Bake for 10–12 minutes until crisp.

7. Leave to cool for 2–3 minutes on the baking sheet, then transfer to a wire rack to cool completely. Cookies can be stored in an airtight container for up to 1 week.

COCONUT & CHOCOLATE MELTS

These crisp, short cookies are great with ice cream. Roll out the dough in batches as it is quite dry and will crack if you try to roll it out all in one go.

MAKES **20–24 COOKIES**

100g plain flour
25g cornflour
75g icing sugar
40g desiccated coconut
1 tablespoon cocoa powder, sieved
110g butter, diced

1. Preheat the oven to 190°C/gas mark 5.

2. Mix together the flour, cornflour, icing sugar, coconut and cocoa powder. Rub in the butter until you have a fine breadcrumb mixture. With your hands bring the mixture together to form a ball.

3. Divide the dough into two and, on a floured surface, roll out one piece to a thickness of 3mm.

4. Stamp out with a cookie cutter and place on a non-stick baking sheet. Bake in batches for 6–8 minutes.

5. Leave to harden up for a couple of minutes before cooling on a wire rack.

CHOCOLATE MACAROONS

Rich, chewy and utterly delicious. If you really want to gild the lily you could sandwich the macaroons with a vanilla buttercream, but I think they are sublime as they are.

MAKES 12–14 MACAROONS

120g plain chocolate
    (50% cocoa solids),
    broken into pieces
100g caster sugar
130g ground almonds
1 teaspoon vanilla extract
2 egg whites
melted white and plain chocolate,
    to decorate (optional)

1. Preheat the oven to 180°C/gas mark 4. Melt the chocolate over a pan of hot water or in the microwave for 1–2 minutes. Leave to cool for a minute or two.

2. Stir in the remaining ingredients, then, with an electric whisk, beat for 2 minutes.

3. Line a large flat baking sheet with non-stick baking parchment. Place tablespoons of the mixture about 7cm apart and bake for 12–15 minutes. Cool on a wire rack, then decorate by piping with white and plain chocolate, if liked.

CHOCOLATE REBELS

The cocoa powder and oats make these cookies really rich and filling.
Best served with a pitcher of really cold milk.

MAKES 24 COOKIES

150g rolled oats
200g self-raising flour
30g cocoa powder, sifted
130g soft brown sugar
100g caster sugar
Pinch of salt
150g unsalted butter, melted
1 egg, beaten
4 tablespoons milk
1 teaspoon vanilla extract
Melted plain chocolate, to decorate
  (optional)

1. Preheat the oven to 180°C/gas mark 4.

2. In a large bowl mix together the oats, flour, cocoa powder, sugars and salt.

3. In another bowl mix together the melted butter, egg, milk and vanilla extract.

4. Pour the wet ingredients into the dry ones and mix well.

5. Place tablespoons of the cookie mixture at regular intervals, but not too close together, on a non-stick baking sheet and bake in the preheated oven for 12–15 minutes.

6. Turn onto a wire rack to cool completely. If liked, decorate with piped plain chocolate.

CHOCOLATE TIP
To decorate cookies or cakes with piped chocolate, melt some chocolate (see page 12) and spoon into a small piping bag or small freezer bag. If using a plastic bag, push the chocolate into the corner and snip of tip. Gently squeeze out the chocolate.

THUMBPRINT COOKIES

These cookies are light and incredibly crumbly with a rich slick of chocolate filling the centres.

MAKES 14–16 COOKIES

125g unsalted butter,
    slightly softened
60g caster sugar
1 egg, beaten
60g plain flour
60g self-raising flour
50g ground almonds
1 tablespoon cocoa powder, sifted
1 tablespoon cornflour
Pinch of salt
FOR THE FILLING
75g plain chocolate
    (50% cocoa solids),
    broken into pieces
2 tablespoons vegetable oil

1. Preheat the oven to 180°C/gas mark 4.

2. Cream together the butter and sugar until light and fluffy. Beat in the egg.

3. Mix the remaining cookie ingredients and gently work into the butter mixture. Refrigerate for 1 hour to harden up – it makes it easier to roll into balls.

4. Take tablespoons of the dough and form into balls. Press firmly with your thumb to make deep indentations in the centres. Place on a non-stick baking sheet and bake for 10–12 minutes until firm. Place on a wire rack to cool.

5. When the cookies have cooled, melt the chocolate in a bowl over a pan of hot water or in the microwave for 1–2 minutes. Cool a little, then stir in the oil. Pour a teaspoon of chocolate into the centre of each cookie and leave to harden.

CHOCOLATE MADELEINES

Try and get hold of a madeleine tray – most good cookshops sell them.
It is essential to always chill a madeleine batter as the texture alters
during the resting time.

MAKES 9 MADELEINES

45g unsalted butter, melted, plus
    extra for greasing the tray
2 eggs
60g caster sugar
55g plain flour
2 tablespoons cocoa powder
1 teaspoon baking powder

1. Grease the madeleine tray with a little melted butter. Whisk the eggs and caster sugar until really thick and pale, the whisk should leave a trail.

2. In a separate bowl sift together the flour, cocoa powder and baking powder. Fold half the flour mixture into the eggs followed by half the butter. Repeat with the remaining flour and butter.

3. Cover and chill for 30 minutes. Preheat the oven to 200°C/gas mark 6.

4. Fill the moulds with the batter and bake for 8–10 minutes until risen and firm to the touch. Leave to cool on a wire rack.

CHOCOLATE TIP
*Try to find silicone moulds,
as it is easier to pop out the
cooked madeleines.*

CHOCOLATE SANDWICH COOKIES

Here's a pretty contrast – the dark richness of the cocoa cookies
is tempered by the mellow flavour of the vanilla buttercream filling.

**MAKES 24 COOKIES
(12 SANDWICH COOKIES)**

225g unsalted butter
120g granulated sugar
275g self-raising flour
55g cocoa powder
2 tablespoons milk
FOR THE FILLING
115g butter
115g icing sugar
1 teaspoon vanilla extract

1. Preheat the oven to 180°C/gas mark 4. Grease a baking sheet and set aside.

2. Cream the butter and sugar in a bowl until light and creamy. Sift in the flour and cocoa powder, then add the milk and mix everything together.

3. With slightly damp hands, shape the dough into walnut-sized balls. Place on a greased baking sheet and press down with the back of a fork.

4. Bake in the oven for 15–20 minutes. Leave to cool on a wire rack.

5. For the filling, beat the butter, sugar and vanilla extract together until smooth and creamy. Once the biscuits are cold, spread a little butter icing on the flat base and sandwich together.

WHITE CHOCOLATE FINGERS

These crisp, buttery Viennese fingers are dipped in white chocolate but you could dip them in some plain or milk chocolate, if you prefer.

MAKES 18 FINGERS

120g unsalted butter,
   slightly softened
40g icing sugar, sifted
1 teaspoon vanilla extract
120g plain flour
100g white chocolate,
   broken into pieces

1. Preheat the oven to 180°C/gas mark 4.

2. Cream the butter, sugar and vanilla extract until light and fluffy. Work in the flour with a wooden spoon until you have a smooth dough.

3. Spoon the mixture into a piping bag fitted with a 2cm wide, fluted nozzle. Pipe out 7.5cm long fingers onto a non-stick baking sheet. Leave a 5–7.5cm gap between the biscuits to allow them to spread.

4. Bake for 10–12 minutes until they are lightly golden. Leave them on the baking sheet for a few minutes to harden up before removing to a wire rack to cool completely.

5. Melt the chocolate in a bowl over a pan of hot water or in the microwave for 1–2 minutes. Dip each end of the cooled biscuits in the melted chocolate and place on non-stick baking parchment until hard.

NO-BAKE CHOCOLATE BARS

These bars are incredibly easy to make and also incredibly rich – so are best cut into small squares to serve.

MAKES 8–10 SQUARES

35g soft brown sugar
140g sweetened condensed milk
45g unsalted butter, slightly softened
180g smooth peanut butter
80g digestive biscuits, crushed

FOR THE TOPPING

225g plain chocolate (50% cocoa solids), broken into pieces
2 tablespoons vegetable oil

1. Line a 19cm square cake tin with non-stick baking parchment.

2. Place the sugar, sweetened condensed milk, butter and peanut butter in a mixing bowl and beat until smooth. Stir in the digestive biscuit crumbs. Spoon into the prepared tin and level the surface. This is easiest done with your hand.

3. Melt the chocolate and oil in a bowl over a pan of hot water or in the microwave for 1–2 minutes. Leave to cool for 5 minutes, then stir.

4. Pour over the surface of the peanut dough and tip the tin to cover evenly. Leave to chill for at least 1 hour. Cut into small squares.

BASQUE CHOCOLATE CAKES

In the bakeries of the Basque region a biscuity sponge filled with a thick custard is a very popular patisserie. Inspired by these morsels, these Basque Chocolate Cakes are a cross between a cake and a biscuit with a delicious surprise of melted chocolate in the centre.

MAKES 12 CAKES

100g plain chocolate
   (70% cocoa solids),
   broken into pieces
60g unsalted butter
100g caster sugar
1 egg, beaten
120g plain flour
2 teaspoons baking powder
12 squares of white chocolate
   (about 55g)
Whipped cream, to serve

1. Melt the chocolate and butter in a bowl over a pan of hot water or in the microwave for 1–2 minutes. Leave it to cool for 5 minutes.

2. Whisk the caster sugar and egg until light and fluffy, then stir in the cooled chocolate mixture. Mix together the flour and baking powder and fold into the chocolate. Cover and chill for at least 1 hour.

3. Preheat the oven to 170°C/gas mark 3. Lightly grease a shallow, 12-cup muffin tin. Divide the dough in two. Take a heaped teaspoon of the chilled dough and press into the base of a muffin cup. Repeat for the remaining muffin cups.

4. Press a square of chocolate into the centre of each cup, then cover with a teaspoon of dough, pressing around the edges to seal. Bake in the oven for 15 minutes, or until the cakes are firm to the touch. Remove and serve warm with some whipped cream.

DOUBLE-CHOCOLATE CHUNKY BROWNIES

Try not to overcook these moreish brownies, otherwise the soft, gooey texture will be spoiled.

MAKES ABOUT 20 SQUARES

225g butter, diced, plus extra
for greasing
500g plain chocolate
1 teaspoon instant coffee granules
1 tablespoon hot water
3 large eggs
175g caster sugar
1 teaspoon vanilla extract
100g self-raising flour
175g pecan nuts, broken into pieces
Cocoa powder, for dusting

1. Preheat the oven to 190°C/gas mark 5. Grease and line a 20 x 30cm cake tin with greaseproof paper.

2. Chop 175g of the chocolate into chunks and set aside. Put the rest in a bowl with the butter and melt slowly over a pan of hot water or in the microwave for 1–2 minutes. Stir until smooth, then leave to cool. Meanwhile, dissolve the coffee in the hot water.

3. Lightly whisk the eggs, coffee, sugar and vanilla extract together in a bowl. Gradually whisk in the chocolate and butter mixture, then fold in the flour, nuts and chocolate chunks.

4. Pour into the prepared tin. Bake for 35–40 minutes or until firm to the touch.

5. Leave to cool for 5 minutes, then cut into squares. Cool in the tin before removing from the greaseproof paper. Dust with cocoa powder before serving.

CHOCOLATE & MARSHMALLOW BLONDE BROWNIES

As the brownies cook the chocolate drops to the bottom and the melted marshmallows rise to the top.

MAKES 8–10 SQUARES

160g unsalted butter,
   slightly softened
130g light brown sugar
100g caster sugar
3 eggs
1 teaspoon vanilla extract
150g plain flour
$1/2$ teaspoon salt
130g plain chocolate chips
75g mini marshmallows or
   large ones cut into quarters

1. Preheat the oven to 180°C/gas mark 4. Base-line a 20cm square cake tin with non-stick baking parchment.

2. Beat together the butter and sugar until light and fluffy. Beat in the eggs and vanilla extract. Stir in the flour and salt followed by the plain chocolate chips and marshmallows.

3. Spoon into the prepared tin and bake for 30–35 minutes until the centre feels slightly firm to the touch. Leave to cool completely in the tin, then cut into squares.

MARBLED CHOCOLATE BROWNIES

The slightly salty creaminess of the cream cheese cuts through the sweetness of the chocolate. Don't expect the brownies to be completely cooked through when you take them out of the oven – they will harden up when cold. When you want to eat them, it is best to chill them and then bring them to room temperature.

MAKES 10–12 SQUARES

240g unsalted butter
250g plain chocolate
   (70% cocoa solids),
   broken into pieces
360g caster sugar
4 eggs
90g plain flour
½ teaspoon salt
300g cream cheese

1. Preheat the oven to 180°C/gas mark 4. Base-line a 22cm square cake tin with non-stick baking parchment.

2. Melt the butter and chocolate together in a bowl over a pan of hot water or in the microwave for 1–2 minutes. Cool a little, then stir until smooth.

3. Beat the sugar with three of the eggs until they are just mixed together. Stir in the melted chocolate and butter. Fold in the flour and salt.

4. Beat the cream cheese with the remaining egg. Spoon alternate dollops of the chocolate mixture and cream cheese into the prepared tin, so you have a rough chequerboard, then swirl together for a marbled effect.

5. Bake in the oven for 45–50 minutes or until the batter stops wobbling in the centre. Leave to cool in the tin, then refrigerate until really firm or overnight. Cut into squares and bring to room temperature to serve.

CHOCOLATE & BRAZIL NUT SHORTBREAD

Brazil nuts are one of the richest sources of selenium, so you can feel good about eating this delicious shortbread.

MAKES 8–10 WEDGES

110g unsalted butter
100g caster sugar
200g plain flour
55g Brazil nuts, ground
55g plain chocolate
    (50–70% cocoa solids), grated

1. Preheat the oven to 170°C/gas mark 3.

2. Cream the butter and sugar together until light and fluffy. Work in the flour, ground nuts and grated chocolate until you have fine crumbs.

3. Press the crumb mixture into the base of a 20cm loose-bottomed cake tin and level the surface. Prick with a fork, then bake in the oven for 30–35 minutes.

4. Remove from the oven and score into wedges. Leave to cool completely before lifting out of the tin.

TIP
When creaming butter and sugar, it is helpful to slightly soften the butter first as this will make creaming easier.

NO-BAKE MILK CHOCOLATE CRACKLE SQUARES

A great standby recipe these squares can be rustled up in a matter of minutes. If you are making these for children you might want to leave out the pine nuts.

MAKES 8–10 SQUARES

225g milk chocolate,
   broken into pieces
55g unsalted butter
330g sweetened condensed milk
100g Rice Krispies cereal
35g pine nuts

1. Base-line an 18 x 24cm cake tin or foil tray.

2. Melt the chocolate and butter in a bowl over a pan of hot water or in the microwave for 1–2 minutes. Leave to cool for 10 minutes.

3. Stir in the sweetened condensed milk, then fold in the Rice Krispies and pine nuts. Spoon into the prepared tin, level the surface and leave until hard – don't put the tin in the refrigerator or the Krispies will go soggy.

4. Cut into squares and serve in paper cases or piled on a plate.

CHOC-MINT CUPCAKES

Any dark chocolate with a soft, fondant mint centre would be fine for the icing, but I favour After Eights. These cupcakes will keep in an airtight container, however, they are best eaten within a couple of days of baking.

MAKES 12 CUPCAKES

120g unsalted butter
100g plain chocolate
   (70% cocoa solids)
   broken into pieces
175g caster sugar
2 eggs, beaten
120g self-raising flour
Pinch of salt
Silver balls, to decorate (optional)

FOR THE ICING
175g After Eights or similar
60ml double cream
60g unsalted butter

1. Preheat the oven to 180°C/gas mark 4. Line a 12-cup muffin tin with paper muffin cases.

2. Put the butter and chocolate in a bowl and melt over a pan of hot water or in the microwave for 1–2 minutes. Cool for a minute or two, then stir in the remaining cake ingredients.

3. Spoon a tablespoon of batter into each muffin case. Place the tray in the preheated oven and bake for 25–30 minutes until just firm to the touch. Cool on a wire rack.

4. For the icing, place all the ingredients in a small saucepan and heat gently, stirring until smooth. Leave for a few minutes, then coat each cupcake with a tablespoon of the icing. Leave to harden and, if you like, decorate with silver balls.

CHOCOLATE, COFFEE & WALNUT CUPCAKES

These cupcakes are for the grown-ups. They are moist and dark with a bitter edge of coffee.

MAKES **12 CUPCAKES**

100g plain chocolate
    (70% cocoa solids),
    broken into pieces
3 teaspoons instant coffee
    granules mixed with
    2 tablespoons boiling water
120g unsalted butter
120g dark brown sugar
2 eggs
120g self-raising flour
70g walnuts, finely chopped
Chocolate-covered coffee beans,
    to decorate (optional)
FOR THE ICING
200g icing sugar, sifted
1 teaspoon instant coffee
    granules mixed with
    2 teaspoons boiling water

1. Preheat the oven to 180°C/gas mark 4. Line a 12-cup muffin tin with paper muffin cases.

2. Put the chocolate and coffee liquid in a bowl and melt over a pan of hot water or in the microwave for 1–2 minutes. Leave for a couple of minutes to cool, then stir until smooth.

3. Cream the butter and sugar until light and fluffy and beat in the eggs. Fold in the flour followed by the melted chocolate and finally the walnuts.

4. Place a tablespoon of the batter in each paper muffin case and bake for 20 minutes or until firm to the touch. Leave to cool on a wire rack.

5. For the icing, mix the icing sugar with the coffee liquid and add a little more boiling water – just enough so the icing has the consistency of double cream. Spoon the icing over the cupcakes, tipping them slightly to cover the surface. Decorate with chocolate-covered coffee beans, if liked.

BLUEBERRY & WHITE CHOCOLATE MUFFINS

These muffins are delicious and so easy to make. They are especially good served warm, so heat them gently in the microwave for a few seconds before serving.

MAKES 12 MUFFINS

250g plain flour, sifted
50g ground almonds
1 tablespoon baking powder
75g caster sugar
250ml milk
3 eggs, beaten
100g butter, melted
½ teaspoon vanilla extract
150g blueberries
75g white chocolate, broken
  into small pieces
FOR THE TOPPING
40g slivered almonds
2 tablespoons Demerara sugar

1. Preheat the oven to 200°C/gas mark 6. Line a 12-cup muffin tin with paper muffin cases.

2. Sift the flour, ground almonds and baking powder into a large bowl and stir in the sugar. Lightly beat together the milk, eggs and butter, then gently fold into the flour with the vanilla extract.

3. Mix in the blueberries and white chocolate pieces – the mixture should be quite lumpy so don't be tempted to beat it.

4. Spoon the mixture into the paper cases until they are three-quarters full. Top each one with a few almonds and a little Demerara sugar, then bake until well risen and golden for 20–25 minutes.

5. Remove the muffins from the tin and leave to cool slightly on a wire rack before serving.

CHOCOLATE CHIP MUFFINS

These muffins are even naughtier when served drizzled with melted plain chocolate!

MAKES 15 MUFFINS

350g self-raising flour
Pinch of salt
6 tablespoons caster sugar
125g good-quality plain chocolate chips
55g butter
175g good-quality plain chocolate, broken into pieces
2 eggs, beaten
300ml buttermilk
125ml milk

1. Preheat the oven to 220°C/gas mark 7. Place 15 paper muffin cases into two muffin tins.

2. Mix together the flour, salt, sugar and chocolate chips in a large bowl.

3. Melt the butter and chocolate in a bowl over a pan of hot water or in the microwave for 1–2 minutes, then leave to cool. Whisk in the eggs, buttermilk and milk.

4. Combine the wet and dry ingredients and stir briskly until the flour is moistened. The mixture should appear rough and lumpy. Fill the paper muffin cases about two-thirds full. Bake for 20 minutes until risen and serve.

CHOCOLATE STREUSEL MUFFINS

The key to making good muffins is not to over-mix when combining the wet ingredients with the dry ones. It may not seem possible, but it all mixes beautifully during the cooking.

MAKES 10–12 MUFFINS

200g self-raising flour
2 teaspoons baking powder
2 tablespoons cocoa powder
Pinch of salt
80g soft brown sugar
2 eggs, beaten
150g plain chocolate
   (50% cocoa solids)
60ml vegetable oil
170ml milk
FOR THE STREUSEL TOPPING
40g soft brown sugar
40g plain flour
1 tablespoon cocoa powder, sifted
25g unsalted butter

1. Preheat the oven to 190°C/gas mark 5. Line a 12-cup muffin tin with paper muffin cases.

2. To make the streusel topping, mix the sugar, flour and cocoa powder together and rub in the butter. Set aside.

3. Mix together the flour, baking powder, cocoa powder, salt and soft brown sugar.

4. Melt the chocolate in a bowl over a pan of hot water or in the microwave for 1–2 minutes. Leave to cool.

5. Beat the eggs into the cooled melted chocolate along with the oil and milk. Pour the chocolate mixture into the dry ingredients and stir 3 or 4 times.

6. Spoon into the muffin cases and sprinkle generously with the streusel mixture. Bake for 15–20 minutes until just firm to the touch. Cool on a wire rack.

CHOCOLATE-COVERED DOUGHNUTS

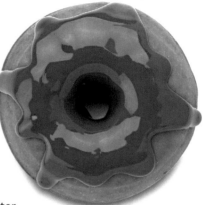

This is a classic bakery favourite. Why not try to re-create it at home – it's easier than you think!

MAKES 8 DOUGHNUTS

225g plain flour
7g sachet fast-action dried yeast
Pinch of salt
50g caster sugar
24g butter
150ml milk
2 egg yolks
Oil, for deep-frying
50g milk chocolate,
    broken into pieces

1. Mix the flour with the yeast and salt. Add the caster sugar, then rub in the butter until the mixture resembles fine breadcrumbs.

2. Heat the milk until it is warm. Whisk in the egg yolks, then add the liquid to the flour. Mix to form a soft dough. Cover the bowl with clingfilm and leave in a warm place for about an hour or until the dough has doubled in size.

3. Knock back the dough on a well-floured surface for 5–10 minutes. Roll out the dough to 1cm thick and stamp out rounds with a plain pastry cutter. Make a hole in the middle of each round with your finger. Place the doughnuts on a greased tray and leave to double in size.

4. Deep-fry the doughnuts in hot oil for about 5 minutes or until they are golden brown. Drain on kitchen paper and leave to cool.

5. Melt the chocolate in a bowl over a pan of hot water or in the microwave for 1–2 minutes. Leave to cool slightly.

6. Dip the rounded tops of the doughnuts in the melted chocolate and leave to harden.

CHOCOLATE BRIOCHE LOAF

Brioche, beloved by the French, is a rich, slightly sweet bread.
Delicious served at breakfast or at teatime.

MAKES 8–10 SLICES

250g strong plain flour
Pinch of salt
50g caster sugar
2 teaspoons (about 8g)
   fast-action dried yeast
55g unsalted butter
2 eggs, beaten
50ml warm milk
55g plain chocolate morsels
FOR THE GLAZE
1 egg beaten with
   1 tablespoon water

1. Mix together the flour, salt, sugar and yeast. Heat the butter in a small saucepan until it has just melted but don't let it boil. Leave it to cool a little.

2. Mix the eggs and warm milk together and pour into the flour followed by the cooled butter. Bring the mixture together to form a smooth dough and knead by hand for 10 minutes or with a dough hook in a food processor or blender for 5 minutes.

3. Turn into a lightly oiled mixing bowl, cover with oiled clingfilm and leave to rise in a warm place for about an hour or until it has doubled in size.

4. Preheat the oven to 200°C/gas mark 6. Grease a fluted brioche mould.

5. Turn the dough out onto a floured surface and knock out the air. Knead in the chocolate morsels. Shape into a round and place in the well-buttered brioche 1.2 litre mould. Leave to rise in a warm place for 15–20 minutes.

6. Brush the surface with a thin layer of the egg glaze, then bake in the oven for 15 minutes. Turn the heat down to 180°C/gas mark 4 and continue to bake for a further 15 minutes.

7. Leave to cool in the tin for 5 minutes, then turn out onto a wire rack to cool completely.

CHOCOLATE CINNAMON SWIRL LOAF

This is a rich freeform dough with veins and swirls of chocolate and cinnamon running through it giving it just a touch of sweetness.

MAKES 10–12 SLICES

600g strong plain flour
1 teaspoon salt
100g caster sugar
4 teaspoons fast-action
  dried yeast
300ml milk
75g unsalted butter
3 eggs, beaten
100g plain chocolate
  (70% cocoa solids), grated
2 teaspoons ground cinnamon
40g soft brown sugar
FOR THE GLAZE
130g icing sugar, sifted
30g cocoa powder, sifted

1. Mix together the flour, salt, caster sugar and yeast in a large mixing bowl.

2. Put the milk and butter in a saucepan and heat slowly until the butter has melted but don't let the milk boil. Cool a little, then stir in the beaten eggs.

3. Add the warm liquid to the flour mixture and bring everything together to form a smooth dough. Either knead by hand for 10 minutes or with a dough hook in a food processor or blender for 5 minutes.

4. Turn into a large, lightly oiled mixing bowl, cover with oiled clingfilm and leave to rise in a warm place for about an hour or until it has doubled in size.

5. Mix together the grated chocolate, cinnamon and soft brown sugar. Turn the risen dough out onto a well-floured surface, knock out the air and knead for 5 minutes.

6. Roll out the dough to a large rectangle about 40 x 25cm. Scatter the grated chocolate mixture over the surface, then roll up to form a long sausage. Curl the sausage into a snail shape and lay in the base of a 25cm buttered cake tin.

7. Preheat the oven to 200°C/gas mark 6. Leave the dough to rise in a warm place for 15–20 minutes, then bake in the oven for 15 minutes.

8. Reduce the heat to 170°C/gas mark 3 and continue to bake for 25–30 minutes. The dough should sound hollowed when tapped. Leave in the tin for 10 minutes, then turn out onto a wire rack to cool completely.

9. When the bread is cold make the glaze. Mix the icing sugar and cocoa powder together and stir in 1–2 tablespoons hot water. The glaze should be the consistency of double cream. Drizzle over the surface of the loaf, letting it drip down the sides.

TIP
Using a dough hook attached to a food processor takes the effort out of bread making, it takes slightly less time and still gives excellent results. Whether kneading the dough by hand or using a dough hook, you are looking for a dough that is smooth, elastic and no longer sticky. Kneading dough is the most critical stage of bread making. It is when the gluten in the flour is activated.

EASY PAIN AU CHOCOLAT

Perhaps not the real McCoy but delicious all the same – quick, easy and the perfect accompaniment to a hot cup of tea as a mid-morning snack or to a scoop of vanilla ice cream as a dessert.

MAKES 6 PASTRIES

225g ready-made puff pastry, preferably all-butter
12 squares plain chocolate (50% cocoa solids), about 100g
1 egg, beaten
2 tablespoons icing sugar, sieved

1. Roll out the dough into a rectangle 27 x 35cm. Cut into three strips lengthways, then cut across the middle horizontally so you end up with six rectangles about 10 x 18cm.

2. Place two squares of chocolate just above the middle of each rectangle and bring the bottom edge up to the top edge. Then fold the two edges back down to the middle. Turn the pastries over and place on a baking sheet lined with non-stick baking parchment. Chill for 15 minutes. Preheat the oven to 180°C/gas mark 4.

3. Brush the pastries with beaten egg and dust with the icing sugar. Bake for 15–20 minutes until puffed up and golden. Leave to cool for 10 minutes before serving.

CHOCOLATE PANETTONE

Panettone is a sweet Italian bread traditionally flavoured with candied fruit and raisins. Here plain chocolate morsels are also added for an extra rich treat. As the dough has so much butter incorporated it takes nearly double the time to rise, so allow plenty of time.

MAKES 12–16 SLICES

500g strong plain flour
1 teaspoon salt
100g caster sugar
2 teaspoons (about 9g)
   fast-action dried yeast
Grated rind of 2 oranges
2 eggs beaten with 2 egg yolks
100ml warm milk
175g unsalted butter, softened
55g candied peel, diced
75g plain chocolate morsels
55g raisins

1. Line a deep 20cm cake tin with baking parchment that comes 5cm above the top of the tin.

2. Mix together the flour, salt, sugar, yeast and orange rind. Mix the eggs with the warm milk and pour into the flour mixture. Stir well and bring together to form a smooth dough. Gradually beat in the softened butter. This is easiest done in a food processor with a dough hook. Knead for 5–10 minutes.

3. Place the dough in a lightly oiled mixing bowl, cover with oiled clingfilm and leave to rise and double in size. This will take about 2 hours.

4. Turn the dough out onto a floured surface and knock out the air. Knead in the candied peel, chocolate morsels and raisins. Form into a round and place in the cake tin. Leave for 50–60 minutes to rise. Preheat the oven to 200°C/gas mark 6.

5. Bake the panettone in the oven for 15 minutes, then turn the heat down to 180°C/gas mark 4 and bake for a further 35–40 minutes. If the dough starts to brown too much cover with a piece of aluminium foil.

6. Leave to cool in the tin for 10 minutes, then turn out onto a wire rack to cool completely.

CHOCOLATE BANANA BREAD

A quick and easy bread, which is delicious served on its own or with butter, to rustle up for a teatime treat. Make sure the bananas are really ripe or the flavour won't be so good.

MAKES 12–14 SLICES

200g plain flour
2 teaspoons baking powder
½ teaspoon salt
1 teaspoon ground mixed spice
100g unsalted butter
150g caster sugar
2 eggs, beaten
1 teaspoon vanilla extract
3 ripe bananas (about 500g), mashed
100g plain chocolate morsels

1. Preheat the oven to 180°C/gas mark 4. Grease and baseline a 1kg loaf tin.

2. Mix together the flour, baking powder, salt and ground mixed spice.

3. Cream the butter and sugar until light and fluffy. Beat in the eggs and vanilla extract followed by the mashed bananas. Fold into the flour mixture and then fold in the chocolate morsels.

4. Spoon into the prepared tin and bake for 1½ hours or until the loaf feels firm to the touch.

5. Leave to cool in the tin for 20 minutes, then turn out onto a wire rack to cool completely. This bread will keep for 4–5 days in an airtight container.

THE PATISSERIE

CHOCOLATE & RASPBERRY ROULADE

This is a perfect afternoon tea treat – just sweet and creamy enough to keep you going through the rest of the day.

MAKES 6–8 SLICES

175g good-quality plain chocolate,
  broken into pieces
100ml water
1 tablespoon instant coffee granules
5 eggs, separated
150g caster sugar
200ml double cream, whipped
150g fresh raspberries
Icing sugar, for dusting

1. Preheat the oven to 200°C/gas mark 6. Line a large 22 x 32cm Swiss roll tin with non-stick baking parchment.

2. Melt the chocolate, water and coffee in a bowl over a pan of hot water or in the microwave for 1–2 minutes. Leave to cool slightly.

3. Combine the egg yolks and caster sugar and whisk until thick and fluffy. Stir in the melted chocolate. Beat the egg whites to soft peaks and carefully fold into the chocolate mixture.

4. Pour into the Swiss roll tin and bake in the oven for 10–12 minutes until firm. Turn out onto another piece of baking parchment and cover with a damp tea towel. Leave to cool.

5. Spread the whipped cream over the sponge, evenly scatter the raspberries on top and roll up. Dust with icing sugar just before serving.

CHOCOLATE CHIP CHIFFON CAKE

A chiffon cake is characteristically baked in a deep ring mould. It is light and airy – a bit like an angel food cake.

MAKES 8–10 SLICES

300g plain flour
1 tablespoon baking powder
½ teaspoon salt
300g caster sugar
6 eggs, separated,
   plus 1 extra egg white
90ml vegetable oil
140ml water
1 teaspoon vanilla extract
½ teaspoon cream of tartar
200g plain chocolate chips

1. Preheat the oven to 170°C/gas mark 3. Liberally grease a deep savarin ring mould or kugelhopf mould with butter.

2. In a large bowl mix together the flour, baking powder, salt and sugar. Mix together the egg yolks, oil, water and vanilla extract, then stir into the flour mixture. Beat for 1 minute.

3. Whisk the egg whites with the cream of tartar until stiff but not dry. Fold into the batter along with the chocolate chips.

4. Pour into the prepared tin and bake for 50–55 minutes or until firm to the touch. Turn onto a wire rack to cool completely.

CHOCOLATE PRALINE TORTE

MAKES 8–10 SLICES

FOR THE PRALINE
225g blanched almonds
125g caster sugar

FOR THE TORTE
175g plain chocolate
   (50% cocoa solids),
   broken into pieces
120g unsalted butter
4 eggs, separated
90g caster sugar
40g plain flour

FOR THE ICING
220ml double cream
15g unsalted butter
200g praline-flavoured milk
   chocolate (e.g. Guylian shells),
   broken into pieces

NOTE
*This recipe makes more praline
than you will need in the recipe.
However, it keeps well in an
airtight container.*

1. Preheat the oven to 190°C/gas mark 5. Grease and base-line a 20cm springform cake tin.

2. For the praline, place the almonds in a large frying pan and toast over a gentle heat, turning frequently for 4–5 minutes until golden. Set aside.

3. Place the sugar and 4 tablespoons water in the frying pan and over a very low heat let the sugar dissolve. Turn the heat up slightly, add the almonds and allow the mixture to cook until a golden caramel colour. Immediately pour onto an oiled baking sheet and leave to cool and harden.

4. Roughly break up the praline and place in a food processor or blender. Keep a few shards aside for decoration. Pulse until you have fine breadcrumbs.

5. For the torte, melt the chocolate and butter over a pan of hot water or in the microwave for 1–2 minutes. Leave to cool a little, then stir to combine.

6. Beat together the egg yolks and sugar until light, thick and the whisk leaves a trail. Fold in the chocolate mixture, 100g praline and then the flour.

7. Whisk the egg whites until they form soft peaks. Fold into the chocolate mixture, then pour into the prepared tin. Bake for 25–30 minutes or until just firm to the touch. Take out of the oven and leave to cool in the tin.

8. For the icing, heat the cream and butter in a pan and just as it is coming up to the boil add the chocolate. Stir until the chocolate has melted then leave to cool. Chill until quite cold, then beat until the mixture is stiff and holds its shape. Cover the torte with the icing, sprinkle with roughly chopped praline and chill until firm.

CHOCOLATE PRUNE CAKE

This is a very moist, flourless cake that will keep well for 4–5 days.

MAKES 8–10 SLICES

150g plain chocolate
(50% cocoa solids),
broken into pieces
45g unsalted butter
250g stoned prunes, puréed with a
couple of tablespoons hot water
4 eggs, separated
55g caster sugar
Whipped cream, to serve

1. Preheat the oven to 180°C/gas mark 4. Grease and base line a 20cm springform cake tin.

2. Melt the chocolate and butter in a bowl over a pan of hot water or in the microwave for 1–2 minutes. Cool a little and then stir in the prune purée.

3. Whisk the egg yolks with the sugar until light and fluffy and thick. Fold the chocolate and prune mixture into the egg yolks.

4. Whisk the egg whites to soft peaks and fold into the chocolate. Pour into the prepared tin and bake for 30 minutes or until firm to the touch.

5. Leave to cool in the tin, then turn out. Serve with whipped cream.

WHITE CHOCOLATE, PEAR & ALMOND CAKE

You could use dried cherries or blueberries instead of the nuts, if you prefer.

MAKES 8–10 SLICES

1 ripe pear
175g unsalted butter,
   slightly softened
180g caster sugar
3 eggs
2 teaspoons vanilla extract
190g plain flour
1 teaspoon baking powder
150g white chocolate, finely chopped
75g blanched almonds,
   roughly chopped
Icing sugar, for dusting

1. Preheat the oven to 180°C/gas mark 4. Grease and base-line a 20cm cake tin.

2. Peel and core the pear and cut into eighths.

3. Cream the butter and sugar together until light and fluffy. Gradually beat in the eggs and vanilla extract.

4. Fold in the flour and baking powder, and finally the white chocolate and almonds.

5. Spoon the cake mixture into the prepared tin and level the surface. Place the pears in a circle on top, pressing them down into the batter. Bake for 45–50 minutes or until risen and firm in the centre.

6. Leave to cool in the tin for 10 minutes before removing and cooling on a wire rack. Dust with icing sugar to serve.

SACHERTORTE

This famous Austrian cake originates in Vienna, where all the cafés claim to make the best one. Some recipes call for almond essence, but I prefer not to use it.

MAKES 8–10 SLICES

175g plain chocolate
 (70% cocoa solids),
 broken into pieces
120g unsalted butter
190g sugar
5 eggs, separated
120g plain flour
FOR THE GLAZE
3 tablespoons apricot jam
FOR THE ICING
140g caster sugar
110g plain chocolate
 (70% cocoa solids),
 broken into pieces
6 tablespoons water

1. Preheat the oven to 160°C/gas mark 3. Line a 20cm cake tin with non-stick baking parchment.

2. Melt the chocolate in a bowl over a pan of hot water or in the microwave for 1–2 minutes.

3. Beat the butter and sugar together, then beat in the egg yolks. Stir in the melted chocolate.

4. Beat the egg whites to soft-peak stage and carefully fold into the chocolate mixture.

5. Sift the flour over and fold in trying to keep as much air as possible in the mixture. Spoon into the prepared tin and bake for 40–45 minutes or until a skewer inserted into the middle comes out clean. Leave to cool in the tin, then place on a wire rack.

6. For the glaze, heat the apricot jam with a tablespoon of water and pass through a sieve if it is lumpy. Cool a little, then brush the glaze over the cake.

7. For the icing, place the icing ingredients in a saucepan and heat through until the sugar has dissolved and the chocolate melted. Then turn the heat up and boil until the temperature reaches 105°C on a sugar thermometer, just below jam stage. Remove from the heat and stir for 1 minute. Pour evenly over the cake. Smooth round the sides with a palette knife, but don't touch the top or it will lose its glossy sheen.

CHOCOLATE KUGELHOPF

A kugelhopf is normally a yeasted bread eaten for breakfast in Germany. Here it is a marbled cake, which is baked in the traditional fluted dome-shaped mould. It is quite a light, dry cake, which is why it is so popular for breakfast.

MAKES 8–10 SLICES

100g plain chocolate
   (70% cocoa solids),
   broken into pieces
25g ground almonds
200g plain flour mixed with
   1 teaspoon baking powder
3 eggs
175g caster sugar
1 teaspoon vanilla extract
FOR THE ICING
130g icing sugar, sifted
30g cocoa powder, sifted

TIP
This cake is easily doubled and you can use the same sized tin (see picture). Increase the cooking time by 45 minutes. Test if cooked with a skewer, which should come out clean – it may need another 5 minutes.

1. Preheat the oven to 150°C/gas mark 2 and liberally butter a 1.5 litre kugelhopf mould.

2. Melt the chocolate in a bowl over a pan of hot water or in the microwave for 1–2 minutes. Leave to cool slightly, then stir.

3. Mix the ground almonds with the flour. Beat the eggs, sugar and vanilla extract until very light and bulky, about 5 minutes.

4. Carefully fold in the flour mixture trying to keep as much air in the batter as possible. Pour in the chocolate and stir – just a couple of times to get a marble effect.

5. Spoon into the prepared mould and bake for 30 minutes or until firm to the touch.

6. Leave to cool for 10 minutes in the mould, then turn out onto a wire rack to cool completely.

7. Mix the icing sugar and cocoa powder together and add just enough hot water to get a thick pouring consistency. Drizzle over the cake.

SOURED CREAM CHOCOLATE CAKE

To ring the changes I like to bake this in a loaf tin. You can cover the cake in an icing of your choice but I happen to like it plain.

MAKES 12–14 SLICES

200g plain chocolate
   (60% cocoa solids or a mixture
   of half 50% and half 70%),
   broken into pieces
120g unsalted butter,
   slightly softened
130g caster sugar
3 eggs
220g soured cream or crème fraîche
150g plain flour
1 teaspoon baking powder
Pinch of salt
Icing and chocolate leaves,
   to decorate (optional)

1. Preheat the oven to 170°C/gas mark 3. Grease and base line a 1kg loaf tin with non-stick baking parchment.

2. Melt the chocolate in a bowl over a pan of hot water or in the microwave for 1–2 minutes. Leave to cool slightly, then stir.

3. Cream the butter and sugar until light and fluffy. Beat in the eggs, then stir in the soured cream or crème fraîche and the melted chocolate.

4. Mix the flour and baking powder together with the pinch of salt and fold into the batter.

5. Spoon the mixture into the tin, level the surface and bake in the oven for 40–45 minutes or until a skewer inserted into the middle comes out just clean.

6. Leave to cool in the tin for 15 minutes, then turn out onto a wire rack. Either leave plain or cover with icing. If covered with icing decorate with chocolate leaves, if liked (see page 13).

CHOCOLATE POUND CAKE

A lot of the recipes in this chapter are very dense chocolaty cakes, but this one is a light, hint-of-chocolate cake. I like to drizzle a little glacé icing over the top to serve.

MAKES 8–10 SLICES

100g plain chocolate
  (50% cocoa solids),
  broken into pieces
220g unsalted butter, softened
230g caster sugar
4 eggs
160g plain yogurt
1 teaspoon vanilla extract
280g self-raising flour
Glacé icing (optional) (see page 154)

1. Preheat the oven to 170°C/gas mark 3. Grease and base-line a 20cm cake tin.

2. Melt the chocolate in a bowl over a pan of hot water or in the microwave for 1–2 minutes. Leave to cool a little.

3. Cream the butter and sugar together until light and fluffy. Beat in the eggs followed by the yogurt, vanilla extract and melted chocolate. Fold in the flour.

4. Spoon the mixture into the loaf tin and bake for 50–55 minutes or until a skewer inserted into the middle comes out clean.

5. Leave to cool in the tin for 10 minutes, then turn out onto a wire rack to cool completely. When cold drizzle with icing if you liked.

WHITE CHOCOLATE CAPPUCCINO CAKE

White chocolate can be a bit sickly but the bitterness of the coffee cuts through the sweetness. I think it works best sandwiched with slightly sweetened whipped cream, but you could use an icing of your choice.

MAKES 6–8 SLICES

130g white chocolate,
   broken into pieces
3 tablespoons milk
150g unsalted butter,
   slightly softened
140g light brown sugar
3 eggs
2 teaspoons instant coffee granules
   mixed with 2 tablespoons boiling
   water
175g self-raising flour
150ml double cream
10g icing sugar, plus extra for dusting

1. Preheat the oven to 180°C/gas mark 4. Grease and base-line two 18cm sandwich tins.

2. Melt the chocolate with the milk in a bowl over a pan of hot water or in the microwave for 1–2 minutes. Leave to cool a little, then stir.

3. Cream the butter and sugar together until light and fluffy. Gradually beat in the eggs and then the coffee liquid.

4. Stir in the melted chocolate. Mix well and then finally, fold in the flour.

5. Divide the mixture between the two prepared tins and bake for 20–25 minutes until golden and firm to the touch. Turn out onto a wire rack and leave to cool.

6. When the cake has cooled, whip together the cream and icing sugar until it is holding its shape and spread over one half of the cake. Top with the remaining half and dust the top liberally with icing sugar.

CHOCOLATE CHESTNUT CAKE

This rich, intense, flourless cake could just as well be served as a pudding.
Just add whipped cream to serve.

MAKES 8–10 SLICES

250g plain chocolate
(70% cocoa solids),
broken into pieces
120g unsalted butter
5 eggs, separated
75g soft brown sugar
425ml sweetened chestnut purée

1. Preheat the oven to 180°C/gas mark 4. Grease and base-line a 20cm springform cake tin.

2. Melt the chocolate and butter in a bowl over a pan of hot water or in the microwave for 1–2 minutes. Leave to cool slightly, then stir until the mixture is smooth.

3. Beat the egg yolks with the sugar until thick. Stir into the melted chocolate mixture followed by the chestnut purée.

4. Whisk the egg whites until they are stiff but not dry and fold into the chocolate mixture.

5. Pour into the prepared tin and bake for 40–45 minutes. Leave to cool in the tin.

NO-BAKE CHOCOLATE LAYER CAKE

I use gingernut biscuits here, but you could substitute a digestive or shortbread if you aren't too keen on the flavour of ginger. You could also use a wheat or gluten-free biscuit if you are intolerant.

MAKES 10–12 SLICES

300g plain chocolate
  (50% cocoa solids),
  broken into pieces
120g unsalted butter,
  cut into small pieces
397g can sweetened condensed milk
110g gingernut biscuits or similar,
  roughly broken

1. Base-line a 1-litre loaf tin with non-stick baking parchment.

2. Melt the chocolate in a bowl over a pan of hot water or in the microwave for 1–2 minutes. Leave to cool a little, then stir until smooth.

3. Gradually add the pieces of butter, beating them in until they have melted and the mixture is smooth. Stir in the condensed milk.

4. Pour a third of the chocolate mixture into the base of the tin. Arrange half the broken biscuits in a single layer over the chocolate. Cover with another third of chocolate and repeat with the remaining biscuits. Pour over the rest of the chocolate.

5. Cover with clingfilm and place in the refrigerator to firm up for about 2–3 hours. Loosen the edges of the layer cake with a sharp knife and turn out onto a plate to serve.

CHOCOLATE FUDGE CAKE

A real fudgy treat here that creates quite a focal point with it's many layers of decadence.

MAKES 8 SLICES

175g unsalted butter,
   plus extra for greasing
250g plain chocolate,
   (70% cocoa solids), broken
   into pieces
4 tablespoons water
175g soft brown sugar
4 eggs, beaten
125g self-raising flour
75g ground almonds
Melted milk chocolate,
   to decorate (optional)

FOR THE FILLING

75g cocoa powder
175g soft brown sugar
50g icing sugar
175g unsalted butter, melted
4 tablespoons boiling water

FOR THE ICING

125g plain chocolate,
   broken into pieces
50g unsalted butter

1. Preheat the oven to 180°C/gas mark 4. Grease and base-line two 18cm cake tins.

2. Melt the chocolate with the water in a bowl over a pan of hot water or in the microwave for 1–2 minutes. Leave to cool slightly.

3. Cream the butter and sugar together until light and fluffy. Gradually add the beaten eggs. Stir in the melted chocolate, then fold in the flour and ground almonds. Pour into the prepared cake tins.

4. Bake for 25 minutes. Leave to cool a little, then turn out both cake halves onto a wire rack. With a long sharp knife, slice them through the middle horizontally so you have four layers.

5. For the filling, mix the cocoa powder, brown sugar and icing sugar together. Beat in the melted butter and stir in the water to make a smooth paste. Leave to harden in the refrigerator for about 20 minutes, then spread evenly over three layers of the cake and sandwich together. Put the final cake layer on top.

6. For the icing, melt the plain chocolate and butter together in a bowl over a pan of hot water or in the microwave for 1–2 minutes. Beat until glossy, then leave to cool until you have a spreading consistency. Smooth evenly over the top of the cake. Drizzle melted milk chocolate over in zigzag patterns, if liked.

SOFT & GOOEY CHOCOLATE CAKE

This is a cake that is best made 24 hours in advance as it needs to firm up a bit before serving.

MAKES 10–12 SLICES

250g plain chocolate (70% cocoa solids), broken into pieces
225g unsalted butter
80g golden syrup
5 eggs
175g caster sugar
55g plain flour
Creme fraîche or soured cream, to serve

1. Preheat the oven to 150°C/gas mark 3. Grease and base-line a 23cm springform cake tin with non-stick baking parchment.

2. Melt the chocolate, butter and golden syrup in a bowl over a pan of hot water or in the microwave for 1–2 minutes. Cool a little, then stir until smooth.

3. In a large bowl stir together the eggs, caster sugar and flour just until the mixture is smooth. Stir in the cooled chocolate mixture. Pour into the prepared tin.

4. Bake for 25–30 minutes – the cake will still have a slight wobble in the middle. Remove from the oven and leave in the tin to cool.

5. Remove the sides of the springform tin but leave the cake on its base and chill for at least an hour. It should be firm enough to slip off the base of the tin. Bring to room temperature and serve with crème fraîche or soured cream.

CHOCOLATE POLENTA CAKE

The polenta in this flourless cake gives it a lovely texture. You can also use fine semolina if you can't find fine polenta.

MAKES 10–12 SLICES

225g plain chocolate
 (60% cocoa solids),
 broken into pieces
60g unsalted butter
5 eggs, separated
120g caster sugar
110g fine polenta
Cocoa powder, for dusting
Icing sugar, for dusting

1. Preheat the oven to 180°C/gas mark 4. Grease and base-line a 23cm springform cake tin.

2. Melt the chocolate with the butter in a bowl over a pan of hot water or in the microwave for 1 2 minutes. Leave to cool slightly, then gently stir until smooth.

3. Whisk the egg yolks with half the sugar until pale and bulky, then stir in the chocolate mixture. Sprinkle the polenta over the mixture and fold in.

4. Whisk the egg whites with the remaining sugar until stiff peaks form, and then fold into the cake batter. Pour into the prepared tin and bake for 25–30 minutes or until slightly firm to the touch.

5. Leave in the tin to cool, then turn out. Dust with cocoa powder and icing sugar to serve.

HAZELNUT MERINGUE LAYER CAKE

MAKES 8–10 SLICES

6 eggs, separated
350g caster sugar
1 teaspoon wine vinegar
160g ground hazelnuts,
   lightly toasted
350g plain chocolate
   (50% cocoa solids),
   broken into pieces
130g icing sugar, sifted
580ml whipping cream
Caramel sauce (optional)
Cocoa powder, for dusting

TIP
*This cake can also be
served as a pudding. You can
make and assemble it in advance,
then freeze it whole. Defrost
at room temperature
for 4–5 hours.*

1. Preheat the oven to 130°C/gas mark ½. Line three baking sheets with non-stick baking parchment and mark out a 20cm diameter circle on each.

2. Beat the egg whites until stiff then beat in half the caster sugar a tablespoon at a time. Fold in the remaining caster sugar followed by the vinegar and ground hazelnuts.

3. Evenly distribute the meringue between the drawn-out discs and level the surfaces so you have three flat discs. Bake in the oven for 1–1½ hours. Remove and place the discs on a wire rack to cool completely.

4. Melt the chocolate in a bowl over a pan of hot water or in the microwave for 1–2 minutes. Leave to cool a little.

5. Place the egg yolks in a large mixing bowl and whisk in the icing sugar until the mixture has doubled in bulk. Stir in the cooled chocolate.

6. Whisk the cream until it is just holding its shape and stir in a couple of tablespoons to soften up the chocolate mixture. Fold in the rest and then chill until the mousse is firm enough to spread, about 2 hours.

7. Spoon half of the chocolate over one meringue disc and smooth to the edges. Lay another meringue disc on top and repeat with the remaining chocolate mousse. Top with the final disc and dust with cocoa powder. If liked, drizzle over each layout of chocolate mousse your favourite caramel sauce. Chill for 1 hour before serving or wrap and freeze.

CHOCOLATE CRATER CAKE

This is a flourless cake – a sort of sunken soufflé that you can fill with whipped cream.

MAKES 8–10 SLICES

225g plain chocolate
   (70% cocoa solids),
   broken into pieces
110g unsalted butter
4 eggs, separated
130g caster sugar
1 teaspoon bitter almond essence
Cocoa powder, for dusting

1. Preheat the oven to 180°C/gas mark 4. Place a roasting tin of boiling water in the bottom of the oven. Grease and base-line a 20cm springform cake tin.

2. Melt the chocolate and butter in a bowl over a pan of hot water or in the microwave for 1–2 minutes. Leave to cool a little, then gently stir until smooth.

3. Beat the egg yolks, sugar and almond extract until really light and creamy. Fold in the chocolate mixture.

4. Whisk the egg whites until stiff and fold into the chocolate mixture. Pour into the prepared tin and bake for 25–30 minutes.

5. Remove from the oven and leave to cool in the tin. This is a very fragile cake so it is best not to try and remove it from its base. Dust with cocoa powder before serving.

SPICED CHOCOLATE CAKE

This is a dense chocolate cake with a hint of spice. It is delicious sliced and spread with a little butter.

MAKES 10–12 SLICES

150g plain chocolate
   (70% cocoa solids),
   broken into pieces
120g unsalted butter
80g golden syrup
360g plain flour
2 teaspoons baking powder
1 tablespoon ground cinnamon
2 teaspoons ground ginger
½ teaspoon freshly grated nutmeg
2 eggs
100g dark brown sugar
120ml double cream

1. Preheat the oven to 150°C/gas mark 3. Grease and base-line a 23cm square cake tin.

2. Melt the chocolate with the butter and golden syrup in a bowl over a pan of hot water or in the microwave for 1–2 minutes. Leave to cool a little, then stir until smooth.

3. Mix together the flour, baking powder and spices in a bowl.

4. Beat the eggs and sugar together until pale and thick. Stir in the melted chocolate mixture, then fold in the flour. Stir in the double cream.

5. Spoon into the prepared tin and bake for 35 minutes or until a skewer inserted into the middle comes out clean. Leave to cool in the tin for 5 minutes, then turn out onto a wire rack to cool completely.

THE DESSERT TROLLEY

MARSHMALLOW & CHOCOLATE ICE CREAM

This rich, luxurious ice cream is even more indulgent when drizzled with
a rich chocolate sauce.

SERVES 8

250g milk chocolate,
    broken into pieces
200g marshmallows, plus extra
    to decorate (optional)
3 tablespoons water
2 x 400g cartons fresh custard sauce
300ml double cream
Rich dark chocolate sauce
    (see page 148), to serve (optional)

1. Place the chocolate in a heatproof bowl with three-quarters of the marshmallows. Add the water and set the bowl over a pan of hot water or melt in the microwave for 1–2 minutes. Melt the chocolate and stir until smooth, then let it cool a little.

2. Stir the cooled chocolate mixture into the custard sauce. Chop the remaining marshmallows and fold into the mixture, then lightly whip the cream and fold in.

3. Pour the mixture into a 1.2 litre terrine or loaf tin and freeze until hard. You may want to line the bottom of the pan with non-stick baking parchment to make it easier to unmould.

4. To serve, dip the base of the mould in hot water and invert on a serving plate. Cut the ice cream into thick slices, decorated with marshmallows and served with chocolate sauce, if liked.

WHITE CHOCOLATE SEMI-FREDDO

Semi-freddo is an Italian dessert – a light and airy ice cream that is not churned and is eaten just on the point of setting. You can make this a few days in advance, but leave it at room temperature for about 45 minutes before you eat it. However, as with all things containing fresh eggs, remember not to refreeze it.

SERVES 6

200g white chocolate,
    broken into pieces
4 eggs, separated
85g caster sugar
450ml double cream

1. Melt the chocolate in a bowl over a pan of hot water or in the microwave for 1–2 minutes. Leave to cool.

2. Whisk the egg yolks with the sugar until really thick and bulky. Stir a little of the egg yolk mixture into the chocolate, then fold in the rest.

3. In another bowl whisk the cream until it is just holding soft peaks. Stir into the chocolate and egg yolk mixture.

4. Finally beat the egg whites to stiff peaks and fold in. Pour the mixture into a container or into individual serving bowls and freeze for 4–5 hours or until the semi-freddo is on the point of setting.

BITTER CHOCOLATE SORBET

Intensely dark and rich, this will satisfy your chocolate cravings. The chocolate must be a good brand and contain at least 70% cocoa solids or the finished sorbet will suffer as a result.

SERVES 4

225g plain chocolate
  (at least 70% cocoa solids)
225g granulated sugar
25g cocoa powder

1. Put the chocolate in a food processor and blend until finely chopped. Place the sugar and cocoa in a saucepan with 500ml water and slowly bring to the boil, stirring to dissolve the sugar. Simmer for 5 minutes.

2. Pour the chocolate syrup into the food processor and run until the mixture is completely smooth and the chocolate has melted. Pour into a shallow container and allow to cool. Once cool, put in the freezer to harden for 2–3 hours.

3. Remove from the freezer. Blend until smooth in the food processor, then return to the container and freeze until hard.

CHOCOLATE AFFOGATO

Affogato is a wonderful instant dessert – and easy to make to finish any dinner party. Normally a shot of fresh espresso coffee is poured over a scoop or two of vanilla ice cream. Here the addition of a little rich chocolate fudge sauce makes this a real treat.

SERVES 6

1 quantity of sticky chocolate
   fudge sauce (see page 150)
12 scoops good-quality
   vanilla ice cream
6 shots of hot espresso coffee

1. Pour the chocolate sauce into six sundae glasses or pudding bowls.

2. Place 2 scoops vanilla ice cream on top of each and finally pour over the hot coffee. Serve immediately.

TIP
For a double hit of coffee you can substitute the vanilla ice cream for a coffee one. For contrast, add a dollop of whipped cream on the top.

CHOCOLATE CHIP & COCONUT ICE CREAM

This creamy ice cream with a subtle taste of coconut has the delightful contrast of crunchy plain chocolate chips.

SERVES 4

650ml coconut milk
5 egg yolks
180g granulated sugar
200ml whipping cream
150g plain chocolate chips

1. Place the coconut milk in a saucepan and slowly bring to the boil.

2. Meanwhile in a bowl whisk the egg yolks and sugar together. Pour over the hot milk and stir. Strain through a sieve and pour back into the saucepan.

3. Stir over a gentle heat until the custard just coats the back of a wooden spoon. Pour into a bowl, cover and chill.

4. Stir the cream into the chilled custard, pour into a container and freeze just until the ice cream is starting to harden. Whisk really well with a fork to disperse the ice crystals, then stir in the chocolate chips. Freeze until hard.

HOT FUDGE SUNDAE

The story goes that the name sundae is derived from the fact that these ice cream treats were originally served only on Sunday, the Sabbath, as they contained no soda water, a mix associated with alcohol.

SERVES 2

Choice of ice cream, such as
   chocolate or vanilla fudge swirl
Whipped cream, to serve
Chocolate shavings, to decorate
FOR THE HOT FUDGE SAUCE
225g sugar
250ml double or whipping cream
30g butter, cut up
1 tablespoon golden syrup
120g unsweetened plain chocolate,
   broken into pieces
1 teaspoon vanilla extract

1. To prepare the sauce, put the sugar, cream, butter, syrup and chocolate in a heavy-based saucepan and set over a medium-high heat. Bring to the boil, stirring constantly, until the chocolate has melted and the mixture is smooth.

2. Reduce the heat to medium-low and cook for about 5 minutes, stirring frequently. Remove from the heat, stir in the vanilla extract and keep warm.

3. Place 2 scoops ice cream in each of two scallop-edged sundae glasses or any dessert bowl. Spoon over 2 tablespoons fudge sauce and top with a swirl of whipped cream. Sprinkle with chocolate shavings and serve immediately.

CHOCOLATE & GINGER BOMBE

Another easy but impressive dessert. It can be made well in advance, as it will keep for up to one week well wrapped in the freezer.

SERVES 6–8

250g plain chocolate
   (50% cocoa solids),
   broken into pieces
4 knobs of stem ginger with syrup,
   finely chopped
500ml double cream
150g meringues
Toasted flaked almonds, to serve
   (optional)

1. Line a 1.1kg pudding basin with clingfilm.

2. Put the chocolate in a bowl and add 3 tablespoons stem ginger syrup and 100ml cream. Melt over a pan of hot water or in the microwave for 1–2 minutes. Leave to cool slightly, then stir until smooth.

3. Add the chopped ginger to the chocolate and mix well.

4. Lightly whip the remaining cream until it is just holding its shape. Fold into the chocolate mixture.

5. Crush the meringues and fold into the chocolate mixture.

6. Spoon into the pudding basin, cover and freeze for 3–4 hours until hard.

7. To serve, invert onto a serving plate and cut into wedges or slices. Sprinkle with toasted flaked almonds, if liked.

CHOCOLATE & ORANGE MOUSSE

This is a quick and easy dessert to knock up – a perfect end to a mid-week supper. Leave out the alcohol if serving to children.

SERVES 4

225g good-quality plain chocolate,
  broken into pieces
Grated rind and juice
  of 1 large orange
1 tablespoon Grand Marnier
4 eggs, separated
55g icing sugar
150ml double cream
Pared strips of orange rind,
  to decorate (optional)

1. Put the chocolate in a heatproof bowl. Add the orange rind and juice and the Grand Marnier and set over a saucepan of simmering water. Heat until the chocolate has melted, then stir until smooth. Leave to cool.

2. Whisk the egg yolks and icing sugar together until the mixture becomes pale and frothy. Stir into the cooled chocolate mixture.

3. Lightly whip the cream and fold into the mousse mixture. Whisk the egg whites in a clean, grease-free bowl until soft peaks form and carefully fold into the mixture. Pour into four custard cups, individual ramekins, a soufflé dish or a glass bowl and leave to chill for 3–4 hours until set. Decorate with orange rind, if liked.

CHOCOLATE GRANITA

Granita is an Italian ice – deliciously refreshing on a hot day. Bear in mind when making the granita that you need to stir the ice every hour for 4–5 hours to keep it from freezing solid.

SERVES 4

880ml water
360g caster sugar
50g cocoa powder

1. Place all the ingredients in a saucepan and stirring continuously, bring to the boil. Stir until the sugar has dissolved, then take off the heat and leave to cool completely.

2. Pour into a large shallow container and freeze until ice crystals are starting to form around the edges. Stir the mixture around with a fork, bringing the ice crystals into the centre.

3. Return to the freezer. Continue to do this every hour until the granita has set.

DOUBLE-CHOCOLATE MINI ALASKAS

These have a biscuit base in place of the more usual cake base. Use the best-quality ice cream you can find, as it needs to freeze really firmly before being baked. Italian-style cooked meringue is more stable than the usual cold whipped method so it can withstand freezing and then high baking temperatures.

SERVES 4

150g plain chocolate
   digestive biscuits, crushed
40g butter, melted
400ml good-quality chocolate
   chip ice cream
1 flaked chocolate bar, cut into 4
3 egg whites
175g caster sugar
$\frac{1}{2}$ teaspoon vanilla extract
Cocoa powder, for dusting

1. Mix the crushed biscuits with the melted butter. Place an 8cm round pastry cutter on a greased baking sheet and spoon a quarter of the crumbs into it. Press down well, then remove the cutter. Repeat three times to make four bases.

2. Place the sheet in a freezer to firm up, about 30 minutes. Soften the ice cream slightly, then divide between the bases. Top each with a piece of flaked chocolate. Return to the freezer and leave until solid for 1–2 hours.

3. Whisk the egg whites, sugar and vanilla extract until frothy. Place the bowl over a pan of gently simmering water and continue whisking until the meringue is thick and glossy, about 10 minutes. Remove from the heat and continue whisking until cool.

4. Take the bases out of the freezer and cover each completely with the meringue. Return to the freezer and freeze for at least 4 hours.

5. Preheat the oven to 220°C/gas mark 7. Bake until golden for 6–8 minutes. Dust with cocoa powder before serving.

CHOCOLATE & CHERRY CHARLOTTE

You can of course make the chocolate cake and ice cream for this recipe but for a simple yet impressive throw-it-together dessert you can use shop-bought produce. Just make sure they are all the best quality you can afford.

SERVES 6

425g can pitted black
   cherries in syrup
500g best-quality bought
   plain chocolate cake
1 litre good-quality chocolate ice
   cream, softened just enough
   to be easy to scoop

1. Line a charlotte mould or 20cm deep cake tin with clingfilm. Drain the cherries reserving the syrup.

2. Cut the chocolate cake into fingers (about the same size as sponge fingers) and dip each piece into the reserved cherry syrup. Line the base and sides of the mould with the cake, leaving enough cake to cover the top.

3. Spoon half the softened ice cream into the base of the mould in an even layer. Cover with the drained cherries. Layer the remaining ice cream over and top with the reserved fingers of chocolate cake. Cover with clingfilm and freeze for 2–3 hours until hard.

4. To serve, turn out the mould onto a serving plate and leave in the fridge for 15–20 minutes to soften slightly. Cut into wedges.

RICH MOCHA POTS

This dark, sultry take on chocolate mousse is a sophisticated, grown-up dessert. For best results use the finest chocolate you can find and chill the mousse well before serving.

SERVES 6–8

175g plain chocolate,
  broken into pieces
3 tablespoons strong black coffee
15g butter
4 eggs, separated
2 tablespoons brandy
4 tablespoons icing sugar
TO DECORATE
Whipped cream
Grated chocolate or curls

1. Melt the chocolate in a bowl over a pan of hot water or in the microwave for 1–2 minutes. Stir in the coffee and butter until smooth.

2. Remove from the heat and whisk in the egg yolks one by one until the mixture is smooth and glossy. Whisk in the brandy, then set aside to cool and thicken slightly while you are whisking the egg whites.

3. Whisk the egg whites in a non-reactive bowl until stiff. Gradually add the sugar and continue whisking until glossy and thick. Fold into the cooled chocolate mixture.

4. Pour into six or eight small teacups or professional ramekins and chill for 3–4 hours until firm. Top with whipped cream and the grated chocolate or chocolate curls.

NOTE
Recipes using raw eggs should be avoided by infants, the elderly, pregnant women and anyone with a compromised immune system.

CHOCOLATE PUDDING

This pudding was so popular in the 1950s, '60s and '70s that packet mixes became available to make it at home. The pudding was literally child's play to make and everyone used the mixes, but it is just as easy to make an original from scratch.

SERVES 4–6

175g sugar
30g cornflour
¼ teaspoon salt
¼ teaspoon ground cinnamon
  (optional)
375ml milk
125ml whipping cream
55g butter, cut into pieces
90g unsweetened plain chocolate,
  broken into pieces
1 egg
1 teaspoon vanilla extract
TO DECORATE
Whipped cream
Chocolate shavings

1. Stir together the sugar, cornflour, salt and cinnamon, if using, in a large heavy-based saucepan and gradually whisk in the milk and cream.

2. Add the cut-up butter and chopped chocolate and set over a medium heat. Cook until the chocolate melts and mixture thickens, whisking frequently. Bring to the boil and boil for 1 minute. Remove from the heat.

3. Beat the egg in a small bowl. Stir in a spoonful of the hot chocolate mixture, whisking constantly. Slowly pour the egg mixture into the chocolate, whisking constantly to prevent lumps from forming. The mixture will be very thick.

4. Strain the mixture into a large measuring jug pressing to push the it through. Stir in the vanilla extract.

5. Pour or spoon the pudding into dessert dishes or ramekins and leave to cool. Cover and chill for 2 hours or overnight. Serve decorated with whipped cream and a few chocolate shavings on top.

CHOCOLATE PROfiTEROLES

As a luxurious alternative to the classic profiterole, these miniature cream puffs are filled with chocolate cream.

MAKES 12 PROFITEROLES

120g plain flour
1 tablespoon icing sugar
200ml water
75g butter, diced
3 eggs, beaten
300ml double cream
2 tablespoons drinking
   chocolate powder

FOR THE SAUCE

115g good-quality plain chocolate,
   broken into pieces
2 tablespoons golden syrup
25g butter
4 tablespoons water

1. Preheat the oven to 200°C/gas mark 6. Sift the flour and icing sugar into a small bowl. Place the water and butter in a saucepan and heat gently until the butter has melted. Bring to a boil, then remove from the heat and quickly add the flour mixture, beating until smooth. Transfer to a bowl and leave to cool.

2. With a hand-held electric mixer, gradually beat the eggs into the mixture to make cream choux pastry. Fit a piping bag with a plain tip and fill with the paste. Pipe 12 rounds onto a non-stick baking sheet. Bake until puffed and golden – about 18–20 minutes. Make a hole in the base of each profiterole and leave to cool on a wire rack.

3. Whip the cream with the chocolate powder until stiff. Fill a new piping bag with the chocolate cream and pipe carefully into the hole in the base of each individual profiterole.

4. To make the sauce, put the chocolate, syrup, butter and water into a bowl and place over a pan of hot water or in the microwave for 1–2 minutes. Melt the chocolate and stir to mix. To serve, drizzle the warm chocolate sauce over the cream-filled profiteroles.

BLACK-BOTTOM CREAM PIE

SERVES 10–12

115g plain flour
3 tablespoons cocoa powder
2 tablespoons icing sugar
75g chilled butter, diced
1 egg yolk
1 tablespoon cold water
Grated chocolate, to decorate

FOR THE FILLING

4 egg yolks
50g caster sugar
4 teaspoons cornflour
400ml milk
55g plain chocolate
1 tablespoon dark rum

FOR THE TOPPING

$1\frac{1}{2}$ teaspoons powdered gelatine
2 tablespoons cold water
120ml double cream
2 tablespoons dark rum
3 egg whites
40g icing sugar, sifted
$\frac{1}{2}$ teaspoon cream of tartar

1. Sift the flour, cocoa and sugar into a bowl. Rub in the butter until the mixture resembles breadcrumbs. Mix the egg yolk and water, add to the dry ingredients and mix to a firm dough. Knead, wrap and chill for 30 minutes.

2. Put a baking sheet in the oven and preheat to 200°C/gas mark 6. Sift a little extra flour and cocoa onto a surface, roll out the pastry and line a greased 23cm pie tin. Prick the base all over, line with foil and baking beans and bake for 15 minutes. Remove the foil and beans, and bake for 10 minutes more. Leave to cool.

3. For the filling, beat the egg yolks, sugar and cornflour together. Bring the milk to a boil, then pour over the egg mixture, beating. Return to the pan and stir over a low heat until thickened. Remove from the heat and stir in the chocolate until melted followed by the rum. Spoon the mixture into the pie shell. Leave to cool.

4. For the topping, sprinkle the gelatine over the water in a bowl and leave to soak for 5 minutes. Set the bowl over a pan of barely simmering water and stir until dissolved. Leave to cool, but not set. Whip the cream until soft peaks form, then slowly beat in the gelatine and rum. Chill for 30 minutes or until starting to thicken, but not set.

5. Beat the egg whites until stiff. Beat in the icing sugar, a tablespoon at a time, with the cream of tartar, then fold into the cream mixture. Spoon the mixture on top of the pie, chill until set, then decorate.

CHOCOLATE MARQUISE WITH VANILLA CRÈME ANGLAISE

A marquise is a super-rich, firm chocolate mousse – delicious!

SERVES 6–8

300g plain chocolate
   (70% cocoa solids),
   broken into pieces
60ml very strong coffee
120g butter
120g caster sugar
4 egg yolks
400ml double cream
FOR THE CRÈME ANGLAISE
300ml milk
1 vanilla pod, split
4 egg yolks
120g caster sugar

1. Line a 21 x 12 x 6cm loaf tin or terrine dish with clingfilm. Put the chocolate and coffee in a heatproof bowl over a pan of hot water or in the microwave for 1–2 minutes. Heat until the chocolate has melted. Stir and then leave to cool.

2. Beat the butter with 75g of the sugar until pale and fluffy. In a separate bowl, whisk the egg yolks with the remaining sugar until thickened and pale. Lightly whip the cream until it just begins to hold its shape.

3. Beat the melted chocolate into the butter and fold in the egg yolk mixture, followed by the cream. Pour into the loaf tin and chill for 5–6 hours.

4. For the crème anglaise, bring the milk to the boil with the vanilla pod. Beat the egg yolks and sugar together. Add the hot milk, then return the mixture to the pan and stir over a low heat until it starts to thicken.

5. Remove the pan from the heat, leave the crème anglaise to cool, then scrape out the seeds from the vanilla pod and stir into the cold custard. Chill until ready to serve.

6. To serve, turn the mousse out onto a serving plate and serve with the vanilla crème anglaise.

WHITE CHOCOLATE PARFAIT

This heavenly little dessert may look innocent enough, but it will appeal to your most devilish instincts!

SERVES 4

175g good-quality white
   chocolate, broken into pieces
2 tablespoons milk
1 vanilla pod
4 egg yolks
75g icing sugar
300ml double cream
TO SERVE
Rich Chocolate Sauce or
   Easy Chocolate Sauce
   (see page 154) (optional)
Fresh cranberries (optional)

1. Melt the chocolate with the milk in a heatproof bowl over a pan of hot water or in the microwave for 1–2 minutes. Leave to cool.

2. Split the vanilla pod lengthways and scrape out the seeds. Mix the seeds with the egg yolks and the icing sugar, then whisk with a hand-held electric mixer until light and fluffy. Stir in the melted chocolate.

3. Lightly whip the cream and fold into the mixture. Divide the mousse between four custard cups, ramekins or dariole moulds and freeze for a minimum of 4 hours until firm.

4. To serve, briefly dip the base of the moulds into warm water and invert on serving plates. Serve with a chocolate sauce and fresh berries such as cranberries, if liked.

KAHLÚA & CHOCOLATE TRIFLE

This variation on the classic tiramisù is very rich and totally addictive!

SERVES 4–6

125ml strong fresh coffee
4 tablespoons Kahlúa
125g sponge fingers
6 tablespoons caster sugar
2 teaspoons vanilla extract
450g mascarpone cheese
250ml double cream
250g plain chocolate, grated
Cocoa powder, for dusting

TIP
For a different flavour experience, use hazelnut liqueur instead of Kahlúa. Coffee and nut make an excellent combination.

1. Grease and line a 1kg loaf tin with clingfilm. Mix the coffee and Kahlúa together. Dip the sponge fingers into the mixture and use a third of them to line the base of the tin.

2. Whisk the sugar and vanilla extract into the mascarpone with an hand-held electric mixer. Add the cream, a little at a time, whisking on a slow speed until smooth.

3. Spoon half of the mixture on top of the sponge fingers and spread evenly. Add half the grated chocolate, then repeat with a layer of the dipped fingers, the remaining cream mixture, grated chocolate and a final layer of dipped sponge fingers. Drizzle any remaining coffee mixture over the top.

4. Cover with a layer of clingfilm, then chill for 2–3 hours. Remove from the tin and peel off the clingfilm. Dust with a generous amount of cocoa powder, slice and serve.

WHITE & DARK CHOCOLATE CHEESECAKE

With a creamy soft texture and delicious chocolate flavour, these cute little cheesecakes will leave you begging for just one more!

SERVES 2

75g digestive biscuits, crushed
45g butter, melted
1 tablespoon unsweetened
   cocoa powder

FOR THE FILLING

75g white chocolate
75g full-fat cream cheese
6 tablespoons crème fraîche
   or soured cream
2 tablespoons icing sugar

TO DECORATE

75g raspberries
25g plain chocolate curls
   or grated plain chocolate
1 tablespoon unsweetened
   cocoa powder

1. Mix together the biscuit crumbs, butter and cocoa. Use two 8cm round cookie cutters to shape the base. Place the cutters on a flat plate and divide the crumb mixture between each of them. Press down on the crumbs until firmly packed.

2. Alternatively, you can line the base of two large ramekins with the crumb base. Place in the refrigerator to chill while you make the filling.

3. For the filling, melt the chocolate in a bowl over a pan of hot water or in the microwave for 1–2 minutes.

4. Beat together all the ingredients for the filling and pour on top of the bases. Chill for 2 hours or until firm.

5. Lift off the cookie cutters, top with raspberries, chocolate curls or the grated chocolate and dust with cocoa.

CHOCOLATE & STRAWBERRY PAVLOVA

Chocolate and berries are a perfect combination and come together beautifully in this moreish meringue dessert.

SERVES 6–8

4 egg whites
Pinch of salt
225g caster sugar
1 tablespoon cornflour
50g plain chocolate,
   broken into pieces
Pinch of ground cinnamon
FOR THE FILLING
300ml double cream
50g milk chocolate, broken up
2 tablespoons milk
225g strawberries, hulled and halved

1. Preheat the oven to 110°C/gas mark ¼. Draw an 18cm circle on a piece of non-stick baking parchment and place ink-side down on a baking sheet.

2. Whisk the egg whites with the salt until stiff. Gradually whisk in the sugar and beat until very glossy and thick. Fold in the cornflour, chopped chocolate and cinnamon.

3. Spoon the meringue mixture into the middle and spread to the circle perimeter, hollowing out the middle slightly.

4. Cook for 1–1½ hours. Set aside to cool, then transfer the meringue to a serving plate.

5. For the filling, lightly whip the cream. Melt the chocolate with the milk over a gentle heat and leave to cool slightly. Roughly fold the chocolate into the cream, leaving it a little streaky. Pile the cream into the centre of the pavlova and arrange the strawberries on top.

MISSISSIPPI MUD PIE

This is a classically rich dessert that will make a perfect end to any special meal.

SERVES 6–8

75g butter, softened
140g plain flour
2 tablespoons iced water
75g chopped walnuts
115g icing sugar
225g cream cheese, softened
500ml double cream, whipped
175g packet instant chocolate
    pudding mix
1 litre milk
1 heaped teaspoon cocoa powder
TO DECORATE
Sifted cocoa powder
Chopped nuts

1. Preheat the oven to 180°C/gas mark 4.

2. Put the butter and flour in a mixing bowl and rub together lightly until the mixture resembles fine breadcrumbs. Stir in the water. Distribute the walnuts through the mixture, then press the mixture into a 23cm pie dish. Bake for 12–15 minutes. Remove from the oven and leave to cool.

3. Combine the icing sugar, cream cheese and 225g of the whipped cream, reserving the rest for the topping in another bowl. Gently spread the mixture over the first cooked layer. Chill.

4. Prepare the pudding mix with the milk, according to the instructions on the packet, in a separate bowl. Mix in the cocoa powder.

5. Remove the chilled pie from the refrigerator and spread the chocolate pudding mix over the second layer. Top with the reserved whipped cream, dust with a fine layer of cocoa powder and sprinkle with chopped nuts. Chill for a further 4 hours before serving.

DARK CHOCOLATE & TOFFEE TART

This dark and mysterious tart is quite rich so is best cut into small slices and served with some crème fraîche as an accompaniment.

SERVES 6–8

275g plain flour,
    plus extra for dusting
Pinch of salt
25g icing sugar
175g unsalted butter, diced
2 egg yolks
4 tablespoons cold water
Cocoa powder, for dusting
FOR THE FILLING
125ml water
350g caster sugar
125g golden syrup
240g unsalted butter
250ml double cream
1 teaspoon vanilla extract
115g plain chocolate
    (50% cocoa), grated

1. Sift the flour, salt and icing sugar into a mixing bowl. Add the butter and rub it in until the mixture resembles breadcrumbs. Whisk the egg yolks with the cold water.

2. Make a well in the centre of the flour and pour in the egg mixture and mix together to form a dough. Knead briefly. Wrap in clingfilm and leave to chill for 20 minutes.

3. Roll out the pastry on a lightly floured surface and use to line a 24cm loose-bottomed tart tin. Prick the pastry all over and chill for 10 minutes.

4. Preheat the oven to 190°C/gas mark 5. Line the pastry case with greaseproof paper and fill with baking beans. Bake for 20 minutes or until golden and crisp. Remove the paper and beans and leave to cool.

5. For the filling, put the water in a large saucepan. Add the sugar and golden syrup and cook over a low heat until the sugar has dissolved. Increase the heat and let it bubble for about 10 minutes until the sauce is a deep caramel colour.

6. Add half of the butter together with the cream and vanilla extract and stand back – it will bubble up. Stir until the mixture is smooth. Pour into the pastry case and chill for 2 hours until set and firm.

7. Melt the chocolate with the remaining butter in a heatproof bowl over a pan of hot water or in the microwave for 1–2 minutes. Leave to stand for 15 minutes.

8. Pour the chocolate mixture over the top of the tart, spreading it evenly with a spatula. Chill for at least 1 hour to set, then dust with cocoa powder.

SWEETHEARTS

A perfect dessert for Valentine's Day – or any day of the year that you want to show someone that you love them!

SERVES 2

125g good-quality white chocolate
1 tablespoon golden syrup
1 tablespoon brandy
150ml whipping cream
2 fresh strawberries, to decorate
FOR THE STRAWBERRY SAUCE
125g strawberries, hulled
1 tablespoon icing sugar

1. Break the chocolate into pieces and place in a heatproof bowl with the golden syrup and brandy. Sit the bowl over a pan of simmering water and allow to melt gently, stirring occasionally.

2. Remove the chocolate from the heat and leave to cool slightly. Whip the cream to soft peaks and carefully fold it into the chocolate mixture. Spoon into two 125ml heart-shaped moulds and leave to set in the refridgerator for at least 2 hours.

3. To make the strawberry sauce, blitz the strawberries in a food processor or blender with the icing sugar. Push through a sieve to remove the seeds.

4. Run the knife gently around the edge of each chocolate heart, then carefully turn out of the mould and transfer to a serving plate. Drizzle the strawberry sauce around the hearts and decorate with the strawberries.

CHOCOLATE CRÊPES WITH CARAMELIZED BANANAS & CREAM

When bananas are cooked they take on a much richer, smoother taste and are a perfect accompaniment to these naughty chocolate crêpes.

MAKES 10 CRÊPES

150g plain flour
2 tablespoons cocoa powder
2 tablespoons caster sugar
2 eggs, beaten
200ml milk
100ml water
1 tablespoon oil
FOR THE FILLING
4 bananas, sliced
50g icing sugar
300ml double cream, whipped

1. Mix the flour, cocoa powder and caster sugar together in a large bowl. Add the eggs and slowly pour in the milk and water, beating until you have a smooth batter. Stir in the oil, then leave to rest for 30 minutes.

2. Brush a large crêpe pan with a little oil and place over medium heat. Pour in a ladleful of batter and fry until set. Flip the crêpe over and quickly fry the other side. Set aside and keep warm. Repeat with the remaining batter.

3. For the filling, place the sliced bananas onto a non-stick baking sheet. Sprinkle with the icing sugar and cook under a preheated grill for 3–4 minutes until golden. Fill each crêpe with a few banana slices and top with a spoonful of whipped cream. Fold the crêpes in half or quarters and serve immediately.

CHOCOLATE BRIOCHE PUDDING

This rich, indulgent pudding is surprisingly good eaten cold the day after baking. However, you may not be able to restrain yourself for that long!

SERVES 8

400g brioche loaf
90g butter
200g plain chocolate
   (70% cocoa solids),
   broken into pieces
300ml half-fat cream
450ml packet instant custard mix
250ml milk

1. With a serrated bread knife, remove the crusts from the brioche, then cut into 1cm slices. Grease a 23cm square gratin dish (or 8 individual gratin dishes) with a little of the butter, then spread the remaining butter sparingly over the brioche. Lay half the slices in the bottom of the dish.

2. Sprinkle half the chocolate evenly over the brioche, then top with the remaining buttered slices. Bring the cream to a boil in a small saucepan, add the remaining chocolate and stir until melted.

3. Whisk the custard and milk together, following the packet instructions, and stir in the chocolate cream. Pour the mixture over the brioche and leave to soak for 30 minutes.

4. Preheat the oven to 150°C/gas mark 2. Place the gratin dish in a bain-marie (baking tin quarter-filled with water) and bake the pudding for 55–60 minutes until firm with a little wobble. Leave to stand for 5 minutes before serving.

CHOCOLATE CREAM PIE

A rich, dark chocolate filling is poured into a buttery pastry shell and chilled until set. Swirls of cream and curls of chocolate make this pie truly decadent.

SERVES 8–10

175g plain flour
2 tablespoons sugar
115g butter, diced
1 egg yolk
2–3 teaspoons cold water
Chocolate curls, to decorate
FOR THE FILLING
50g cornflour
90g caster sugar
160ml single cream
275ml milk
90g milk chocolate,
    broken into pieces
2 egg yolks
2 tablespoons butter
FOR THE TOPPING
240ml double cream
$\frac{1}{2}$ teaspoon vanilla extract
2 teaspoons icing sugar, sifted

1. Sift the flour and sugar into a bowl. Rub in the butter until the mixture resembles fine breadcrumbs.

2. Mix together the egg yolk and 2 teaspoons water and sprinkle over the dry ingredients. Mix to a firm dough, adding the extra water if needed. Lightly knead, then wrap in clingfilm and chill for 30 minutes.

3. Put a baking sheet in the oven and preheat to 200°C/gas mark 6. Roll out the pastry on a lightly floured surface and use to line a shallow 20–23cm pie dish. Chill for 10 minutes.

4. Line the pie shell with baking parchment and baking beans. Bake blind for 15 minutes. Remove the parchment and beans and cook for another 8–10 minutes or until the pie shell is golden and crisp. Remove from the oven and leave to cool on a wire rack.

5. To make the filling, mix the cornflour and sugar in a non-stick pan. Gradually blend in the cream and then stir in the milk and chocolate. Gently heat, stirring constantly until the chocolate melts and the mixture thickens and boils. Remove from the heat.

CHOCOLATE TIP

To make thick chocolate curls, melt 175g milk chocolate with 2 tablespoons pure white vegetable fat, stirring until smooth. Pour into a small pan lined with baking parchment, to produce a thick block. Chill until set. Let the block come to room temperature. Hold the block over a plate and pull the blade of a swivel-bladed peeler firmly along the edge.

6. Beat the egg yolks in a small bowl. Stir in a few spoonfuls of the chocolate mixture, one at a time, then pour the egg mixture back into the chocolate mixture in the pan, stirring constantly. Cook and continue to stir for another 1 minute but do not boil.

7. Remove from the heat and stir in the butter. Cool for a few minutes, then pour into the pie shell. To prevent a skin forming, press a circle of dampened baking parchment onto the surface of the filling. Leave to cool, then chill for 2 hours. Remove the baking parchment.

8. For the topping, pour the cream into a chilled bowl. Stir in the vanilla extract and sugar. Whip until the cream forms soft peaks, then spoon into a pastry bag with a large star nozzle and pipe a lattice pattern on top of the pie. Scatter with chocolate curls and serve.

CHOCOLATE PECAN PIE

The pie is filled with a deliciously fudgy mixture of nuts, chocolate and maple syrup. Delicious warm or cold with a dollop of whipped cream.

SERVES 8–10

225g plain flour
Pinch of salt
4 tablespoons icing sugar, plus extra for dusting (optional)
120g unsalted butter, diced
2–3 tablespoons cold water
Whipped cream, to serve
FOR THE FILLING
225g pecans
150g plain chocolate, roughly chopped
55g unsalted butter, diced
3 eggs
225g soft light brown sugar
185ml maple syrup
1 tablespoon plain flour

1. Sift the flour into a mixing bowl with the salt and icing sugar. Add the butter and using your fingertips, rub the butter into the flour until the mixture resembles coarse breadcrumbs.

2. Add cold water and using your hands, a narrow spatula or a palette knife start to bring the dough together, adding a little more water, if it is necessary.

3. Turn the dough onto a lightly floured surface and knead briefly, just until the dough is smooth. Form into a neat ball, flatten into a disc and wrap in clingfilm. Chill for at least 20 minutes.

4. Remove the pastry from the refrigerator and leave at room temperature for 5–10 minutes. Unwrap and place on a lightly floured surface. Lightly flour the top of the dough and a rolling pin and roll out the pastry to line a 25-cm loose-bottomed tart tin. Prick the base and chill for 10 minutes.

5. Line the pie shell with baking parchment and weigh down with baking beans. Bake in a preheated oven at 180°C/gas mark 4 until golden and crisp – about 20 minutes. Remove the paper and beans.

6. Reduce the oven to 170°C/gas mark 3. Roughly chop three-quarters of the pecans with a large knife and scatter over the cooked pastry case.

7. Melt the chocolate and butter in a bowl set over a pan of hot water or in the microwave for 1–2 minutes. Stir and leave to cool.

8. Whisk together the eggs, brown sugar and maple syrup. Stir in the cooled chocolate and fold in the flour. Pour into the pastry case. Arrange the remaining nuts on top and bake until the centre is just set – about 50–55 minutes.

9. Remove the pie from the oven and allow to cool slightly. Dust with icing sugar, if liked, and serve with whipped cream. If made ahead, reheat in a 150°C/gas mark 2 oven for 5–10 minutes.

THE CHOCOLATERIE

CHOCOLATE TRUFFLES WITH ORANGE FLOWER WATER

For dark chocolate truffles, replace the white chocolate with plain and use brandy instead of the orange flower water.

MAKES **10 TRUFFLES**

80ml double cream
150g white chocolate,
   broken into pieces
1–2 tablespoons orange flower water
4 tablespoons cocoa powder

1. Heat the cream in a small saucepan until almost boiling. Take off the heat and leave to cool for 5 minutes or until warm enough to touch.

2. Stir in the chocolate and orange flower water and mix until smooth.

3. Dust your hands in a little cocoa and put the remainder on a flat plate. Scoop out a walnut-sized piece of chocolate with a spoon and roll it in your hands. Roll in cocoa and put on a clean plate. Repeat with the remaining mixture.

4. Chill for 1 hour to firm up before serving.

SIMPLE CHOCOLATE FUDGE

This is a great recipe for getting the kids involved, as apart from melting the chocolate and butter, it requires no other cooking.

MAKES ABOUT 25 SQUARES

60g unsalted butter
120g plain chocolate
  (70% cocoa solids),
  broken into pieces
360g icing sugar, sifted

1. Line an 18cm square cake tin with non-stick baking parchment.

2. Melt the butter and chocolate in a bowl over hot water or in the microwave for 1–2 minutes. Leave to cool for a couple of minutes, then stir until smooth.

3. Beat half the icing sugar into the melted chocolate and butter and stir in a tablespoon of boiling water. Repeat with the remaining icing sugar and a further tablespoon of boiling water.

4. Spoon the fudge into the tin, level out the surface and refrigerate until hard. Cut into small squares.

TIP
As a delicious variation, add a handful of raisins or chopped nuts to the mixture before you pour it into the tin.

SMOOTH CHOCOLATE & DRIED CRANBERRY FUDGE

It is easiest to make good fudge with a sugar thermometer, but the soft–ball test works well if you are vigilant and test every minute or so. If you can't find dried cranberries you could substitute raisins.

MAKES ABOUT 25 SQUARES

300ml full-fat milk
450g granulated sugar
55g plain chocolate (70% cocoa solids), broken into pieces
30g unsalted butter
75g dried cranberries

1. Line an 18cm square cake tin with non-stick baking parchment.

2. Heat the milk and sugar in a large, heavy-bottomed saucepan, stirring until the sugar has dissolved.

3. Add the chocolate and butter and stir until smooth. Continue to cook, stirring to prevent the mixture burning, until the temperature reaches 115°C. Test the mixture by dropping a tiny bit into a bowl of cold water. If it holds its shape and can be rolled into a soft ball it is ready.

4. Take the saucepan off the heat, add the cranberries and start to beat, for about 4–5 minutes until really thick. Immediately pour into the prepared tin and leave to cool completely. Cut into squares to serve.

CHOCOLATE TOFFEE

A sticky toothsome treat! Successful toffee making is all about the sugar reaching the correct temperature. The easiest way to guarantee success is to use a sugar thermometer.

MAKES ABOUT 36 PIECES

375g Demerara sugar
225g unsalted butter
200g golden syrup
25g cocoa powder

1. Line a 20 x 20cm square cake tin with non-stick baking parchment.

2. Place all the ingredients in a large, heavy-based saucepan and cook slowly, stirring, until the sugar has dissolved.

3. Turn the heat up and bring to the boil until the temperature reaches hard ball stage (120°C) on a sugar thermometer. If you don't have a thermometer drop a little bit of the mixture into a bowl of cold water and if it hardens immediately it is ready.

4. Pour the mixture into the prepared tin and leave until cold and hard. Cut into pieces.

TIP
Don't be afraid to keep testing the toffee with your sugar thermometer to make sure you reach hard-ball stage.

MILK CHOCOLATE & PINE NUT CLUSTERS

Making the caramel is a bit of a fiddle but worth the effort when you bite into the fudgy, nutty centre. Try and get the best milk chocolate – it really makes a difference.

MAKES ABOUT 25 CLUSTERS

175g caster sugar
130ml double cream
240g pine nuts
200g good-quality milk chocolate,
    broken into pieces

1. Line a baking sheet with non-stick baking parchment.

2. Place the sugar in a wide saucepan and heat slowly without stirring. Let the sugar melt without colouring too much. It should be a golden caramel colour.

3. Pour in the cream, being careful as it bubbles up. Stir over a low heat until the caramel is smooth. Take off the heat and stir in the pine nuts. Pour onto the prepared baking sheet and leave to get cool completely.

4. Once the mixture has cooled take spoonfuls and with slightly damp hands roll into balls. Set aside.

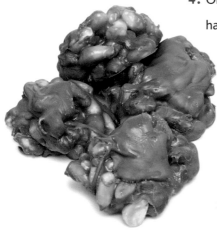

5. Melt the chocolate in a bowl over a pan of hot water or in the microwave for 1–2 minutes. Cool a little. Place a clean sheet of non-stick baking parchment on a board.

6. It is messy but it is easiest to dip the caramel nut clusters into the melted chocolate with your fingers. Place them on the lined board and leave to harden. Serve in petit four cases or simply on a serving dish.

ROCKY ROAD FUDGE

The melted marshmallows give the fudge a creamy texture.

MAKES ABOUT 25 SQUARES

420ml milk
520g granulated sugar
45g unsalted butter
25g cocoa powder
75g marshmallows

1. Line a small square cake tin, about 15 x 15cm, with non-stick baking parchment.

2. In a large, heavy-bottomed saucepan heat the milk and sugar and stir until the sugar has dissolved. Add the butter and cocoa powder and bring to the boil, still stirring.

3. Continue to cook, stirring to prevent the mixture burning, until the temperature reaches 115°C. Test the mixture by dropping a tiny bit into a bowl of cold water. If it holds its shape and can be rolled into a soft ball it is ready.

4. Take the saucepan off the heat and stir in the marshmallows. Beat until the mixture is thick and has lost its gloss.

5. Pour into the prepared tin and leave to cool and harden. Cut into squares to serve.

MINI CHOCOLATE & RAISIN LOGS

If you want to make these at Christmas you could run the prongs of
a fork across the tops of the logs and make little holly like leaves and
berries with coloured marzipan.

MAKES ABOUT 15 LOGS

150g plain chocolate
   (70% cocoa solids),
   broken into pieces
90g unsalted butter,
   cut into small pieces
50g icing sugar, sifted
2 egg yolks
90g raisins
Cocoa powder, for rolling
   and dusting
Icing sugar, for dusting

1. Melt the chocolate in a bowl over a pan of hot water or in the
microwave for 1–2 minutes. Cool a little, then stir in the pieces of
butter, little by little until smooth.

2. Stir in the icing sugar, egg yolks and finally the raisins. Place the
mixture in the refrigerator to harden up.

3. Dust a work surface with cocoa powder and roll spoonfuls of the
chocolate mixture into little logs. Dust with a little more cocoa powder
and a sprinkling of icing sugar before serving.

CHOCOLATE & PEANUT BRITTLE

You really need a sugar thermometer to make brittle, so don't attempt this without one. I coat the brittle in a mixture of plain and milk chocolate, but you could use all plain or all milk chocolate if you have a favourite.

MAKES ABOUT 500G

180g caster sugar
240g golden syrup
200g unsalted peanuts
30g unsalted butter
1 teaspoon bicarbonate of soda
100g plain chocolate
   (70% cocoa solids),
   broken into pieces
100g milk chocolate,
   broken into pieces

1. Grease a 35 x 25cm Swiss roll tin.

2. Place the sugar and golden syrup in a large, heavy-based saucepan and bring to the boil, stirring.

3. When the temperature has reached 140°C, add the peanuts and butter and continue to cook until the temperature reaches 152°C. Take off the heat and add the bicarbonate of soda.

4. Pour into the prepared tin and leave until cold and hard. Break into pieces.

5. Melt the chocolate in a bowl over a pan of hot water or in the microwave for 1–2 minutes. Leave to cool a little, then stir to combine.

6. Dip the ends of the brittle pieces into the melted chocolate, then leave to harden on a sheet of non-stick baking parchment.

BITTER CARAMEL & CHOCOLATE ROCKS

The hint of dark brown sugar gives these candies a sophisticated flavour. Watch the almonds carefully when you are grilling them – they burn very easily.

MAKES **ABOUT 15 ROCKS**

250g blanched whole almonds
35g dark brown sugar
200g plain chocolate
  (70% cocoa solids),
  broken into pieces
1 tablespoon vegetable oil

1. Preheat the grill to its hottest setting. Place the almonds in a food processor or blender and pulse two or three times until the nuts are roughly broken up. Turn onto a non-stick baking sheet, sprinkle the nuts with the sugar and mix well.

2. Cook them under the grill for 3–4 minutes turning them over frequently to ensure even colour. Remove and leave to cool.

3. Melt the chocolate and oil in a bowl over a pan of hot water or in the microwave for 1–2 minutes. Leave to cool a little, then stir until smooth. Stir in the cooled nuts.

4. Either spoon into petit four cases or leave until the mixture has hardened a little and spoon onto non-stick baking parchment. Leave until completely hard.

MILK CHOCOLATE & PISTACHIO TORRONE

Torrone is an Italian nougat full of nuts and candied fruit. It is best not attempted without a sugar thermometer.

MAKES ABOUT 50–60 PIECES

540g granulated sugar
240g honey
3 egg whites
240g shelled, unsalted pistachios
55g candied orange peel,
  finely chopped
200g milk chocolate,
  broken into pieces

1. Line a baking tin, about 24 x 33cm with non-stick baking parchment.

2. Place the sugar and honey in a heavy-based saucepan and slowly bring to the boil, stirring occasionally.

3. Place the thermometer in the liquid and when the temperature is coming up to 140°C, start to whisk the egg whites until stiff. When the temperature of the liquid reaches 160°C (hard crack), take off the heat and pour onto the whisked egg whites, continuing to whisk until the mixture starts to get really tacky and harden around the whisk, about 3–4 minutes. Stir in the nuts and orange peel, then spoon into the prepared tin.

4. Dampen your hands with water and pat down the torrone to the edges of the tin. Cover with a layer of non-stick baking parchment and leave to get cold and hard.

5. Melt the chocolate in a bowl over a pan of hot water or in the microwave for 1–2 minutes. Leave to cool for a minute or two, pour over the torrone and spread to the edges with a spatula. Leave to harden and then cut into squares.

WHITE CHOCOLATE & PRALINE HEARTS

These are great fun to do for Valentine's Day. See the Chocolate Praline Torte recipe (see page 58) for instructions on how to make praline.

MAKES **ABOUT 12 HEARTS**

200g white chocolate,
  broken into pieces
15g unsalted butter
30g crushed praline (see page 58)

1. Place a sheet of non-stick baking parchment on a flat board. Trace around a heart-shaped cookie cutter (about 5–6cm). You should have about 12.

2. Melt the chocolate and the butter in a bowl over hot water or in the microwave for 1–2 minutes. Leave to cool a little, then stir until smooth.

3. Following the shape of the heart spread out spoonfuls of the chocolate. Then leaving a little margin around the edges sprinkle over the praline and press down gently so it sticks into the chocolate.

4. Refrigerate until hard, then peel off the paper. Serve with coffee as an after-dinner sweetie.

TIP
For variety, try making these with plain chocolate or a combination of white and plain chocolate. Proceed as described above.

RICH CHOCOLATE & COFFEE SQUARES

Serve as bite-size treats for after dinner or at a wedding. You could cover them with a coating of glacé icing (see page 154), but I happen to like them plain.

MAKES ABOUT 30 SQUARES

150g plain chocolate
   (70% cocoa solids),
   broken into pieces
120g unsalted butter
2 teaspoons instant coffee
   granules dissolved in
   2 tablespoons boiling water
2 eggs, separated
120g caster sugar
55g ground almonds
40g plain flour

1. Preheat the oven to 180°C/gas mark 4. Grease and base-line a 19x 19cm square cake tin with non-stick baking parchment.

2. Melt the chocolate and butter in a bowl over a pan of hot water or in the microwave for 1–2 minutes. Leave to cool a little, then stir in the coffee. Set aside.

3. Whisk together the egg yolks and sugar until pale and thick. Stir in the cooled chocolate mixture followed by the ground almonds and flour.

4. Whisk the egg whites to soft peaks, then fold into the chocolate. Pour the mixture into the prepared tin and bake for 15 minutes or until just firm to the touch.

5. Leave to cool in the tin, then turn out and cut into small squares.

MINI CHOCOLATE MOUSSE & STRAWBERRY TARTS

MAKES 24 TARTS

FOR THE PASTRY
160g plain flour
1 tablespoon cocoa powder
35g icing sugar, sifted
120g unsalted butter, cut into cubes
1 egg, beaten
FOR THE MOUSSE
175g plain chocolate
(50% cocoa solids),
broken into pieces
3 eggs, separated
3–4 small strawberries, finely sliced,
to decorate

1. Preheat the oven to 180°C/gas mark 4.

2. To make the pastry, mix together the flour, cocoa powder and icing sugar in a bowl. Add the butter and rub in until the mixture resembles fine breadcrumbs. Stir in the egg and enough cold water to bring the mixture together.

3. Roll out the dough thinly on a floured surface and stamp out rounds big enough to line the 12-cup mini tart trays. Prick the bases and chill for 30 minutes.

4. Bake in the oven for 10 minutes until the pastry is cooked. When they have cooled a little remove the pastry cups from the trays and cool on a wire rack.

5. To make the mousse, melt the chocolate in a bowl over a pan of hot water or in the microwave for 1–2 minutes. Cool a little, then stir in the egg yolks. Whisk the egg whites until stiff and fold into the chocolate mixture.

6. When the tarts are cold spoon or pipe the mousse into the tarts and leave in a cool place to set. Serve decorated with slices of strawberry.

CHOCOLATE DIPPED FRUIT

As an alternative dessert put the bowls of freshly prepared fruit on the table and let each person dip their choice of fruit into the melted chocolate. If you are serving it this way, stir 1–2 tablespoons double cream into the melted chocolate beforehand to prevent the chocolate going hard again.

SERVES 4

100g chocolate of your choice
(a mixture of plain and milk
is delicious)
220–300g mixed fruit, such as
strawberries, cherries, cape
gooseberries, grapes, bananas,
pears, ready-to-eat dried figs,
dates or apricots

1. Line a baking sheet with non-stick baking parchment.

2. Melt the chocolate in a bowl over a pan of hot water or in the microwave for 1–2 minutes.

3. With a skewer or toothpick quickly dip the pieces of fruit into the chocolate, allowing the excess to drip off, and place them on the lined baking sheet. Leave to cool.

TIP
This can be prepared a few hours in advance but no longer, as the fresh fruit will start to go soggy and discolour.

CHOCOLATE PEPPERMINT FONDANTS

These are easy fondants that you can make with the children. Try and find authentic peppermint essence and not peppermint flavouring, which can have a very harsh taste.

MAKES ABOUT 25 FONDANTS

450g icing sugar, sifted, plus extra
   for rolling out
1 egg white
A few drops of peppermint essence
100g plain chocolate
   (70% cocoa solids),
   broken into pieces
1 tablespoon vegetable oil

1. Place the sifted icing sugar in a large mixing bowl and work in the egg white, adding a little water to make a smooth paste. Add a few drops of peppermint essence – enough to suit your tastes.

2. Liberally dust a work surface with icing sugar and roll out the paste to a thickness of about 1cm. Stamp out 2.5cm rounds with a cookie cutter.

3. Place the discs on a wire rack and leave to dry out for about 12 hours.

4. Melt the chocolate and oil in a bowl over a pan of hot water or in the microwave for 1–2 minutes. Leave for a minute or two to cool and then stir until smooth.

5. Dip the peppermint discs into the chocolate and place on a piece of non-stick baking parchment to harden.

FRENCH COLETTES

Lining the petit four cases with the melted chocolate is a bit fiddly, but the end results are pretty impressive.

MAKES 16 COLETTES

200g plain chocolate
   (70% cocoa solids),
   broken into pieces
45g unsalted butter
100ml double cream

1. Melt 120g chocolate in a bowl over a pan of hot water or in the microwave for 1–2 minutes. Leave to cool a little, then stir until smooth.

2. Take 16 petit four cases and, one by one, spoon a little chocolate into the bottom. Tip the case around making sure the sides of the case are covered with chocolate. Pour off any excess into the bowl. Place in the refrigerator to harden up. Repeat with the remaining cases.

3. Repeat the whole process a second time. Check the chocolate case is thick enough by peeling off one of the petit four cases. If the chocolate is not thick enough repeat a third time. When the cases have hardened up peel off the paper and refrigerate while you make the filling.

4. Melt the remaining chocolate in a bowl over a pan of hot water or in the microwave for 1–2 minutes. Cool for a minute, then beat in the butter a little at a time until the mixture is smooth. Lightly whip the cream and fold into the chocolate.

5. Let the chocolate filling set slightly (about 5 minutes in the refrigerator), then spoon into a piping bag and pipe into the chocolate cases or spoon the filling directly into the cases, levelling out the top. Leave in the refrigerator to set.

CHOCOLATE PRALINES

These little pralines are light and melting. Unlike European pralines that contain nuts, these are the American versions, which are nut-free.

MAKES ABOUT 25 PRALINES

180g granulated sugar
120g light brown sugar
150ml double cream
45g unsalted butter
75g plain chocolate
   (70% cocoa solids),
   broken into pieces

1. Line a baking sheet with non-stick baking parchment.

2. Place the sugars and cream in a large, heavy-based saucepan and, stirring slowly, bring to the boil. When the mixture reaches soft-ball stage (118°C) take it off the heat and beat in the butter and chocolate.

3. Working quickly drop spoonfuls of the mixture onto the baking parchment. If the mixture becomes too solid add a touch of boiling water. Leave to cool completely.

TIP
As a variation and for a contrast of flavours, drizzle the pralines with melted plain chocolate.

FROZEN ICE CREAM TRUFFLES

You really must buy the best-quality ice cream for these truffles as cheap, soft-scoop ice cream won't hold its shape.

MAKES 12 TRUFFLES

1 small tub best-quality
   ice cream, vanilla or coffee
125g plain chocolate
   (70% cocoa solids),
   broken into pieces
1 teaspoon vegetable oil

1. Working quickly, with a melon baller scoop out 12 balls of ice cream and place on a sheet of baking parchment. Immediately place in the freezer for at least 1 hour.

2. Melt the chocolate in a bowl over a pan of hot water or in the microwave for 1–2 minutes. Leave to cool a little, then stir in the oil.

3. Very quickly dip each ice cream ball into the melted chocolate and replace in the freezer immediately to harden up. Serve with toothpicks as an after-dinner treat.

MINI CHOCOLATE, CARAMEL & COCONUT SQUARES

MAKES ABOUT 36 SQUARES

FOR THE BASE
250g plain digestive biscuits
   or similar
45g unsalted butter, melted

FOR THE CARAMEL
350g sweetened condensed milk
80g desiccated coconut
100g light brown sugar
45g unsalted butter
200g plain chocolate
   (50–70% cocoa solids),
   broken into pieces
2 tablespoons vegetable oil

1. Preheat the oven to 180°C/gas mark 4. Base-line a 19 x 19cm square cake tin with non-stick baking parchment.

2. Finely crush the biscuits and stir in the melted butter. Press into the base of the prepared tin and bake in the oven for 5 minutes. Cool slightly.

3. To make the caramel, place the condensed milk, coconut, sugar and butter in a saucepan and stir over a low heat for 8–10 minutes until thick. Spread the caramel over the biscuit base and cook in the oven for 5–10 minutes. Leave to cool completely.

4. Melt the chocolate in a bowl over a pan of hot water or in the microwave for 1–2 minutes. Leave to cool a little, then stir in the oil. Pour over the caramel, spreading the chocolate to the edges. Leave until hard, then cut into little squares.

MARBLED CHOCOLATE EGG

MAKES 1 EGG

225g best-quality plain chocolate, broken into pieces
120g best-quality white chocolate, broken into pieces
25g melted chocolate to join edges

1. First you need to polish the inside of a 15cm plastic egg mould with a soft cloth. This will help when you come to unmould the chocolate later.

2. Place the chocolates in two separate bowls and melt over pans of hot water or in the microwave for 1–2 minutes. Leave to cool slightly.

3. Drop alternate spoonfuls into each half, tilting the moulds so the chocolates run together and coat the inside of the moulds. Don't put too much chocolate into the moulds – you are going to do at least two layers anyway. Then draw through the chocolate with a skewer so you get a marbled effect. Refrigerate until set.

4. Repeat with a second layer, refrigerate, then repeat again. Refrigerate until the chocolate is completely set.

5. Carefully pull each mould from the chocolate, you may need to ease it out with the point of a knife.

6. To join together the two sides, spread a little bit of the melted chocolate along the edges and press together. Place in the refrigerator until hard.

THE TOPPINGS

EASY CHOCOLATE SAUCE

This sauce is perfect as a storecupboard standby as it takes next to no time
to rustle up and complements a multitude of desserts.

SERVES 4

50g cocoa powder
130g caster sugar
360ml water
30g unsalted butter

1. Place all the ingredients in a saucepan and, stirring gently, bring to the boil.
2. Let the sauce boil for 2 minutes, without stirring, then leave to cool a few minutes before serving.

RICH DARK CHOCOLATE SAUCE

A very indulgent sauce that can be served hot or cold.

SERVES 4

225g plain chocolate
   (70% cocoa solids),
   broken into pieces
75g unsalted butter
190ml double cream

1. Place all the ingredients in a saucepan and stir over a gentle heat until the sauce is smooth and glossy.

WHITE CHOCOLATE FUDGE SAUCE

This can be poured over a dark chocolate sponge as a wonderful contrast. Alternatively, it can double up as a white chocolate fondue – dip in a selection of fresh fruit or pieces of Madeira cake. It is also delicious served drizzled over a fresh fruit salad.

SERVES 6

225g white chocolate,
   broken into pieces
220ml milk
220ml double cream
1 teaspoon vanilla extract
3 teaspoons cornflour mixed
   with 1 tablespoon milk

1. Place the chocolate, milk, cream and vanilla extract in a saucepan and stir over a gentle heat until the chocolate has melted.

2. Stir in the cornflour mixture and cook, stirring for 1–2 minutes until the sauce is thick enough to coat the back of a wooden spoon. Serve warm.

STICKY CHOCOLATE FUDGE SAUCE

This sauce is possibly the most popular sauce and one of the easiest to make with all the ingredients going into the pan at the same time.

SERVES 4–6

225g plain chocolate
   (50–70% cocoa solids),
   broken into pieces
125g soft brown sugar
220ml double cream
30g unsalted butter
1 tablespoon golden syrup

1. Place all the ingredients in a saucepan and stir over a gentle heat until the sauce is smooth. Serve hot.

TIP
For a slightly different flavour try this delicious sauce using maple syrup instead of golden syrup.

CHOCOLATE CUSTARD SAUCE

The perfect accompaniment to a steamed chocolate pudding.

SERVES 4–6

250g soft brown sugar
90g cocoa powder
1 tablespoon cornflour
360ml milk
15g unsalted butter

1. Place the sugar and cocoa powder in a saucepan. In a bowl mix the cornflour with a little of the milk, then pour in the rest of the milk. Pour this into the saucepan.

2. Stir over a gentle heat until the sauce thickens, then whisk in the butter. Serve warm.

EASY CHOCOLATE BUTTERCREAM ICING

Perfect for filling children's fairy cakes.

MAKES ENOUGH TO FILL AND COAT AN 18–20CM CAKE

2 tablespoons cocoa powder, sifted
150g unsalted butter, softened
275g icing sugar, sifted

1. Mix the cocoa powder with a little boiling water to make a smooth paste.

2. Beat the butter until soft and add the cocoa powder. Gradually beat in the icing sugar.

GLACÉ ICING

This icing is suitable for covering cakes and pastries rather than filling them.
It will give a glossy finish to your cake.

MAKES ENOUGH TO COAT AN 18–20CM CAKE

120g icing sugar, sifted
1 tablespoon cocoa powder, sifted

1. Mix together the icing sugar and cocoa powder. Stir in a tablespoon of boiling water and mix until smooth. You may need to add a touch more water to get the right consistency.

2. This icing needs to be used straight away or it forms a crust.

GANACHE FROSTING

A lovely, rich and decadent topping to any dessert.

MAKES ENOUGH TO FILL AND COVER AN 18–20CM CAKE

300g plain chocolate
   (50–70% cocoa solids),
   broken into pieces
200ml double cream
30g unsalted butter,
   cut into small pieces

1. Place the chocolate and double cream in a saucepan and stir over a gentle heat until the chocolate has melted.

2. Stir in the butter. Leave to cool until the mixture has a spreadable consistency.

SOURED CREAM & CHOCOLATE ICING

The soured cream in this icing cuts through the sweetness of the chocolate to lighten it slightly.

MAKES ENOUGH TO FILL AND COAT AN 18–20CM CAKE

200g plain chocolate
  (50% cocoa solids),
  broken into pieces
60g unsalted butter
400ml soured cream or crème fraîche
120g icing sugar, sifted

1. Melt the chocolate and butter in a bowl over a pan of hot water or in the microwave for 1–2 minutes. Leave to cool for a few minutes, then stir until smooth.

2. Stir in the soured cream followed by the icing sugar. Chill until you have a firm enough consistency to ice a cake.

CHOCOLATE TIP

To make marble-effect shards of chocolate, melt equal quantities of plain and white chocolate. Spread the dark chocolate onto a tray lined with non-stick baking parchment until a few millimetres thick. Drizzle over the white chocolate and gently drag it through, making a pattern of your choice. Allow to cool, then break up and use the pieces as decoration.

CHOCOLATE FUDGE ICING

A perfect fudgy topping to any cake – the grainy texture of the frosting provides an especially delightful contrast to a soft sponge.

MAKES ENOUGH TO FILL AND COAT AN 18–20CM CAKE

175g plain chocolate
   (50% cocoa solids),
   broken into pieces
175g unsalted butter
75g soft brown sugar
2 tablespoons double cream
300g icing sugar, sifted

1. Melt the chocolate in a bowl over a pan of hot water or in the microwave for 1–2 minutes. Leave to cool slightly.

2. Place the butter, sugar and cream in a saucepan and stir over a gentle heat until the sugar has dissolved. Stir in the melted chocolate and finally beat in the icing sugar. The mixture will begin to separate. When it does add 3–4 tablespoons boiling water and beat until glossy and smooth.

THE BAR

HOT CHOCOLATE WITH CARDAMOM

If you're in need of a comforting drink, this is the one for you. Warmed milk has been used as the classic bedtime soporific for centuries, and the soothing taste of chocolate and sweetly spiced cardamom are just delicious.

MAKES 2

500ml full-fat milk
4 cardamom pods, bruised
115g plain chocolate,
   broken into pieces
120ml double cream
Cocoa powder or shaved chocolate,
   to decorate (optional)

1. Pour the milk into a pan and add the cardamom pods. Bring almost to the boil, then remove from the heat and leave to steep for 10 minutes.

2. Remove the cardamom pods and return the pan to the heat. Heat gently, until almost boiling, and then whisk in the chocolate until melted. Pour into two large cups or mugs.

3. Whip the cream until it stands in very soft peaks and spoon on top of the hot chocolate. Decorate with cocoa powder or shaved chocolate, if you like.

MEXICAN HOT CHOCOLATE

Mexican chocolate is a mixture of chocolate, ground almonds and spices, sweetened with sugar, and you can buy it in specialist stores. Here you can make your own deliciously aromatic drink.

MAKES 2

550ml full-fat milk
50g ground almonds
45g caster sugar
2 teaspoons ground cinnamon
1 vanilla pod, split down the centre
100g plain chocolate
    (50–70% cocoa solids),
    broken into pieces

1. Place the milk, ground almonds, sugar, cinnamon and vanilla pod in a saucepan and bring to the boil over a gentle heat. Take off the heat and leave to infuse for 20 minutes.

2. Pour the mixture through a very fine sieve into a clean saucepan, squeezing out the milk from the ground almonds.

3. Add the chocolate and stir over a low heat until the chocolate has melted. Serve immediately.

CHOCOLATE MILKSHAKE

MAKES 2 LARGE SHAKES

600ml milk
5 scoops chocolate ice cream
2 tablespoons drinking
    chocolate powder
2 tablespoons ready-made
    chocolate sauce (optional)

1. Place the milk, ice cream and drinking chocolate in a food processor or blender and blend until thick and frothy.

2. Pour the liquid into two tall glasses. Stir in a tablespoon of your favourite chocolate sauce if using.

SUPER-RICH INDULGENT HOT CHOCOLATE

This is definitely a once-in-a-while treat-yourself drink. If you have a slightly sweeter tooth use a chocolate containing 50% cocoa solids.

MAKES 2 GENEROUS MUGS OR 4 SMALL TEACUPS

200ml whipping cream
1 vanilla pod, split down the middle
120g plain chocolate
   (70% cocoa solids),
   broken into pieces
400ml full-fat milk
Whipped cream and grated
   chocolate, to serve

1. Pour the cream into a saucepan, add the split vanilla pod and slowly bring to the boil.

2. Take off the heat and add the broken-up chocolate. Stir until the chocolate has melted and the mixture is smooth then return to a low heat and stir in the milk. Heat through, then remove the vanilla pod.

3. Pour into mugs or teacups and top with a spoonful of whipped cream and a sprinkle of grated chocolate.

HOT MOCHALATTE

A classic combination of coffee and chocolate come together to make this creamy treat.

MAKES 2

2 tablespoons cocoa powder
2 teaspoons instant coffee granules
50g caster sugar
550ml full-fat milk

1. Place the cocoa powder, coffee granules and sugar in a small bowl and pour over 3–4 tablespoons boiling water. Mix to a smooth paste.
2. Heat the milk in a saucepan and whisk in the cocoa paste. Stir over a gentle heat until piping hot.

WHITE CHOCOLATE & STRAWBERRY SMOOTHIE

You could also use raspberries for this smoothie, but you may want to sieve the pips before serving.

MAKES 2

100g white chocolate, broken into pieces
200ml milk
250g strawberries, washed and hulled

1. Put the chocolate and milk into a saucepan and stir over a gentle heat until the chocolate has melted. Leave to cool.
2. Place the strawberries and the cooled milk into a food processor or blender and blend until smooth. Pour into two glasses and serve the smoothies immediately.

ICED CHOCOLATE

This recipe includes milk to make one iced chocolate, although there is enough chocolate syrup here for about ten drinks – but it will keep for at least a week in the fridge.

MAKES 1

450ml water
280g granulated sugar
100g plain chocolate
    (50–70% cocoa solids),
    broken into pieces
40g cocoa powder, sieved
200ml cold milk

1. Place the water and sugar in a saucepan and heat slowly, stirring until the sugar has dissolved. Turn the heat up and boil for 5 minutes.

2. Take off the heat and stir in the chocolate and cocoa powder. Whisk until smooth. Leave to cool completely.

3. Pour about 50ml of the chocolate syrup (or to taste) into a large glass and add the cold milk. Stir well and top up with ice.

CHOCOLATE & MALTED MILK SMOOTHIE

Don't keep this childhood milkshake just for the kids – it's perfect as a wicked evening treat for adults too.

MAKES 2

400ml full-fat milk
200ml whipping cream
4 scoops chocolate ice cream, slightly softened
4 tablespoons Horlicks powder or Ovaltine

1. Place all the ingredients in a food processor or blender and blend until smooth. Serve chilled.

MILK CHOCOLATE & BANANA SMOOTHIE

This creamy smoothie is a bit like a drink version of a banana split – wickedly indulgent. For an extra treat use gold top milk.

MAKES 2

200ml milk
100g milk chocolate,
   broken into pieces
2 bananas
4 scoops vanilla ice cream

1. Bring the milk up to the boil, then take off the heat and whisk in the chocolate. Leave to cool completely.

2. Pour the cooled chocolate milk into a food processor or blender and add the remaining ingredients. Blend until smooth and frothy. Serve the smoothies immediately.

VANILLA STRACCIATELLE SMOOTHIE

A delicious vanilla-flavoured yogurt smoothie coloured with specks of grated chocolate. It is a drinkable version of the Italian ice cream that has strands of chocolate running through it.

MAKES 2

450ml vanilla-flavoured yogurt or
   fromage frais
200ml cold milk
50g milk chocolate, coarsely grated

1. Put the yogurt or fromage frais into a food processor or blender with the milk and blend until frothy.

2. Pour into a jug and stir in the grated chocolate. Serve immediately.

NEW WAYS WITH CHOCOLATE

ROAST PUMPKIN & CHOCOLATE SOUP

I like to roast the pumpkin as it seems to concentrate the flavour of the vegetable.

SERVES 4

1.6kg pumpkin,
   seeds and rind removed
3 tablespoons olive oil
200g red onions, peeled
   and finely chopped
1.5 litres chicken stock
10g bitter chocolate
   (99% cocoa solids), broken up
1 stick of cinnamon
Crème fraîche, to serve
Salt and freshly ground black pepper

1. Preheat the oven to 200°C/gas mark 6. Cut the pumpkin flesh into 5cm pieces, then spread the pieces onto a large baking sheet and spoon over 2 tablespoons of the olive oil. Season with salt and freshly ground black pepper and roast in the oven for 45 minutes.

2. Pour the remaining tablespoon of olive oil into a large saucepan and add the chopped onion. Cook over a low heat for 10–12 minutes until softened but not coloured.

3. Add the roasted pumpkin to the pan and pour in the chicken stock. Add the chocolate and cinnamon stick. Bring to the boil, then turn the heat down and simmer for 20 minutes. Remove the cinnamon stick and leave to cool before liquidizing in a food processor or blender.

4. Taste the soup and season with plenty of salt and freshly ground black pepper. Serve each portion with a spoonful of crème fraîche and an extra sprinkling of freshly ground black pepper, if liked.

ROAST CHICKEN WITH BITTER CHOCOLATE GRAVY

Perfect with roast chicken, Bitter Chocolate Gravy is more of a jus than the thicker traditional gravy. It is quite a strong sauce, so a little goes a long way.

SERVES 4–5

1 lemon, cut into quarters
1 free-range chicken,
    weighing about 1.8kg
Half a head of garlic, separated
    into cloves, unpeeled
1 small bunch of fresh thyme
80g butter, slightly softened
510ml chicken stock
1 tablespoon balsamic vinegar
25g bitter chocolate
    (70% cocoa solids), broken up
Salt and freshly ground black pepper

1. Preheat the oven to 200°C/gas mark 6. Stuff the lemon quarters into the chicken cavity along with the garlic cloves and half the thyme. Smear 55g of the butter over the chicken and season with salt and freshly ground black pepper.

2. Place the chicken in a large roasting tin and cover with foil. Roast for 50 minutes, then remove the foil, baste and continue to cook for 20–25 minutes. The chicken is done when the juices from the centre of the leg run clear. Remove the chicken from the roasting tin, cover with foil and leave to rest for 10–15 minutes.

3. Remove the leaves from the remaining thyme sprigs and chop finely. Pour off the fat from the roasting tin, leaving the juices and add the chopped thyme. Over a high heat add the chicken stock and balsamic vinegar and simmer for 5 minutes. Take off the heat, whisk in the chocolate and stir until smooth.

4. Taste and season with salt and freshly ground black pepper. Whisk in the remaining 25g butter. Serve with the roast chicken.

TURKEY MOLE

You can just as well use cooked turkey in this recipe and in fact it is a great way of spicing up the remains of a Christmas turkey. Simply add the turkey after cooking the tomato sauce for 15 minutes and heat through.

SERVES 4

1 tablespoon vegetable oil
1 onion, peeled and finely sliced
2 sticks celery, finely chopped
2 green peppers, deseeded
  and finely chopped
2 garlic cloves, peeled
  and finely sliced
1 mild green chilli, deseeded
  and finely chopped
1 small dried chilli, crumbled
A couple of pinches of ground cumin
700g turkey breast or leg meat,
  cut into thin slices
375g passata (sieved
  chopped tomatoes)
10g bitter chocolate
  (85% cocoa solids), broken up
Salt and freshly ground black pepper
TO SERVE
1 tablespoon toasted flaked almonds
2 tablespoons chopped fresh
  coriander

1. Heat the oil in a large frying pan with a lid. Add the onion, celery, peppers, garlic and green chilli and cook over a low heat, stirring every now and again, for 15 minutes until the vegetables are soft.

2. Add the dried chilli and pinches of cumin and stir in the sliced turkey. Cook for 5 minutes, stirring.

3. Pour in the passata and season with salt and freshly ground black pepper. Cover and simmer for 15–20 minutes. Stir in the chocolate and taste and season again if necessary.

4. Just before serving sprinkle over the flaked almonds and chopped fresh coriander.

CHILLI CON CARNE

A touch of chocolate adds a velvety richness and a wonderful depth of flavour to the chilli. I don't like it to be fiery hot, but if that is your preference you can up the quantity of dried chillies.

SERVES 4

1 tablespoon vegetable oil
250g onions, peeled
  and finely chopped
3 garlic cloves, peeled and crushed
800g beef mince
2 teaspoons ground cumin
1 teaspoon dried oregano
2 small dried hot chillies, crushed
2 tablespoons tomato purée
1 tablespoon tomato ketchup
330ml beef or chicken stock
1 x 400g can kidney beans,
  drained and rinsed
15g bitter chocolate
  (99% cocoa solids), broken up
Salt and freshly ground black pepper
Soured cream, grated cheese and
  tortilla chips, to serve

1. Heat the oil in a large saucepan, add the onions and garlic and cook over a low heat for 10 minutes until softened.

2. Add the beef mince and turn the heat up. Stirring to break up the mince, brown for 3–4 minutes, then turn the heat down. Add the cumin, oregano and crumbled chillies and cook for a further minute.

3. Stir in the tomato purée and tomato ketchup and then pour in the stock. Simmer the chilli con carne for 45 minutes.

4. Stir in the kidney beans and cook for a further 5 minutes. Stir in the chocolate and taste and season with salt and freshly ground black pepper.

5. Serve with soured cream, grated cheese and tortilla chips on the side.

VENISON & CHOCOLATE CASSEROLE

This is the perfect dish for a cold winter's day – rich and warming. It is preferable to marinate the venison overnight, but if you don't have the time a couple of hours is better than nothing.

SERVES 4–5

500ml red wine
2 garlic cloves, peeled and crushed
2 onions, peeled and finely sliced
2 bay leaves
2 sprigs of fresh rosemary
1 heaped teaspoon juniper berries, finely chopped
6 cloves
2 tablespoons olive oil
2 strips of orange peel
900g shoulder or leg of venison, cut into 4cm pieces
3 large carrots, peeled and sliced into rounds
300ml chicken or vegetable stock
20g bitter chocolate (85% cocoa solids), broken up
3 teaspoons cornflour
Salt and freshly ground black pepper
Chopped fresh parsley, to garnish

1. Put the wine, garlic, onions, bay leaves, rosemary, juniper berries, cloves, olive oil and orange peel into a large bowl. Add the venison and mix well. Cover and leave to marinate overnight.

2. Transfer to a casserole dish and add the carrots and stock. Slowly bring to the boil and season with salt and freshly ground black pepper. Cover and simmer for 2 hours by which time the meat should be very tender.

3. Stir in the chocolate and taste and season again if necessary. Mix the cornflour with 3 teaspoons cold water and stir into the casserole. Heat through until thickened a little. Spoon onto serving dishes and garnish with a sprinkling of chopped parsley.

ROAST RIB OF BEEF WITH CHOCOLATE & MADEIRA SAUCE

I think a rib of beef is the tastiest joint. It may not be as tender as a fillet, but the flavour wins hands down. Make sure the meat is at room temperature before roasting it, as it will affect the cooking time if it comes straight out of the refrigerator.

SERVES 4

1 tablespoon vegetable oil or dripping
1 onion, peeled and cut into eighths
1 carrot, peeled and roughly chopped
4 garlic cloves, unpeeled
1.8kg rib of beef, bone-in
1 tablespoon plain flour
90ml Madeira
480ml beef or chicken stock
10g bitter chocolate
   (99% cocoa solids), broken up
Salt and freshly ground black pepper

1. Preheat the oven to 200°C/gas mark 6. Pour the oil or dripping into a roasting tin and add the onion, carrot and garlic cloves. Place the meat on top of the vegetables and season well with salt and freshly ground black pepper.

2. Roast for 60–80 minutes depending on how rare you like your meat. Lift out the beef, cover with foil and leave to rest for 10–15 minutes.

3. Pour off all but a tablespoon of fat from the roasting tin, keeping the vegetables. Stir in the flour and cook over a low heat for a minute. Slowly whisk in the Madeira and cook for 3–4 minutes until thickened.

4. Add the stock and simmer, stirring, for a further 3–4 minutes. Add the chocolate and stir until melted. Taste and season if necessary.

5. Strain the sauce through a sieve squeezing out as much juice as you can from the vegetables.

6. Carve the meat and serve the sauce separately.

ROAST PHEASANT WITH SALSA AGRODOLCE

A salsa agrodolce is a sweet-sour sauce that here is enriched with a touch of bitter chocolate.

SERVES 6

3 small hen pheasants
50g butter, softened
Small bunch of fresh thyme
Salt and freshly ground black pepper
2 tablespoons chopped fresh thyme,
   to serve

FOR THE SALSA AGRODOLCE
10g butter
1 onion, peeled and finely chopped
2 tablespoons caster sugar
3 tablespoons red wine vinegar
180ml red wine
150ml chicken stock
10g bitter chocolate
   (80% cocoa solids), broken up
25g unsalted butter

1. Preheat the oven to 200°C/gas mark 6. Place the pheasants in a large roasting tin and rub over the butter. Stuff each cavity with the thyme sprigs and season well with salt and freshly ground black pepper. Roast for about 50–55 minutes or until a skewer inserted into the leg joint feels piping hot. Remove from the oven, cover and leave to rest for 10 minutes.

2. While the pheasants are roasting you can make the salsa agrodolce. Melt the butter in a small saucepan and add the onion. Cook slowly for 10 minutes until the onions are softened but not coloured. Spoon into a bowl and set aside.

3. In the same pan add the caster sugar and red wine vinegar. Over a gentle heat stir until the sugar has dissolved, then turn the heat up and boil until the liquid has reduced to almost nothing. Pour in the wine and stock, add the reserved onions and simmer for 15 minutes. Take off the heat and whisk in the chocolate followed by the unsalted butter. Taste the sauce and season with salt and plenty of freshly ground black pepper.

4. Serve slices of the pheasant with a little sauce and chopped thyme scattered over to finish.

CHORIZO, WHITE BEAN & CHOCOLATE RAGOÛT

A great time-saving alternative is to use three 400g tins of drained cannellini beans in place of the dried beans – simply add them at step 4.

SERVES 4

320g dried cannellini beans
½ onion, peeled
1 stick of celery
5 sprigs of fresh thyme
1 bay leaf

FOR THE RAGOÛT

3 tablespoons olive oil
2 medium-sized onions, peeled and finely chopped
1 carrot, peeled and finely diced
2 cloves garlic, finely chopped
400g can chopped tomatoes
210ml red wine
360ml chicken stock or water
1 tablespoon chopped fresh rosemary, plus 4 extra sprigs, to serve
320g chorizo sausage, skin removed and sliced into 5mm discs
10g bitter chocolate (99% cocoa solids), broken up
Salt and freshly ground black pepper

1. Put the dried beans into a large bowl and fill with cold water. Leave to soak overnight.

2. Drain the beans and put in a large saucepan with the onion, celery, thyme and bay leaf. Fill the saucepan two-thirds full with cold water. Bring to the boil, then turn the heat down and simmer for 45–50 minutes or until the beans are soft. Drain and set aside.

3. To make the ragoût, wipe out the pan and add the olive oil, chopped onions, carrot and garlic. Cook over a low heat for 10 minutes until the vegetables have softened but not coloured. Add the chopped tomatoes, wine, stock or water and chopped rosemary. Bring to the boil, then turn the heat down and simmer for 10 minutes.

4. Add the cooked beans and chorizo and cook for a further 15 minutes. Take off the heat and stir in the chocolate.

5. Taste the ragoût and season with salt and freshly ground black pepper. Spoon into four serving bowls and garnish each with a sprig of rosemary.

BAKED HAM WITH CHOCOLATE GLAZE

This is an interesting and delicious alternative to the traditional honey and mustard glaze for ham. I prefer this version served cold with a crunchy salad and baked potato.

SERVES 6

2.7kg piece of unsmoked gammon,
    bone-in
1 onion
1 stick of celery
1 carrot, peeled and halved
1 teaspoon whole cloves

FOR THE GLAZE

150g soft brown sugar
90ml cider vinegar
60ml ginger wine
40g plain chocolate
    (70% cocoa solids), broken up
Pinch of ground cloves
Salt and freshly ground black pepper

1. Put the gammon into a large saucepan and cover with water. Bring to the boil and then remove from the heat and drain.

2. Cover with cold water and add the onion, celery, carrot and cloves. Bring to the boil, then turn the heat down and simmer for 2 hours.

3. Meanwhile, make the glaze. Put the sugar, vinegar and ginger wine into a saucepan and slowly bring to the boil. Simmer for 5 minutes.

4. Take off the heat and whisk in the chocolate. Season with a little salt and freshly ground black pepper and stir in the ground cloves.

5. Preheat the oven to 200°C/gas mark 6. Drain the gammon and put it in a large roasting tin.

6. Pour the chocolate glaze over the gammon. Roast in the oven for 20 minutes, basting the joint every 5 minutes with the chocolate glaze. Remove from the oven and leave to rest for 10–15 minutes before serving.

CHOCOLATE & PEPPERED STEAK

Try and find some flavoursome, well-hung meats for this dish. Fillet steak may be the most tender, but it is often lacking in flavour.

SERVES 2

2 x 200g sirloin steaks
    at room temperature
1 teaspoon sunflower oil
1 tablespoon crushed black
    peppercorns
5g bitter chocolate
    (99% cocoa solids), grated
Salt

1. Put the steaks onto a plate and brush with the oil. Press the peppercorns evenly over both sides and season with salt.

2. Heat a frying pan until hot and fry the steaks for 1–2 minutes each side, depending on their thickness and how well-done you like them.

3. Remove the steaks to serving plates and sprinkle over the chocolate. Leave to rest for a couple of minutes, then serve.

TIP
Never be afraid to let any meat, red or white, rest. It allows it to relax as the juices disperse, and this helps the meat to retain its moisture.

CHOCOLATE, TOMATO & CHILLI PASTA

SERVES 4

400g 00 flour (available
    in most supermarkets)
10g cocoa powder
4 eggs
Grated parmesan, to serve
FOR THE TOMATO CHILLI SAUCE
2 tablespoons olive oil
2 garlic cloves, peeled
    and finely chopped
1 tablespoon rosemary leaves,
    finely chopped
2 x 400g cans chopped tomatoes
1 dried chilli, crumbled
Pinch of caster sugar
Small bunch of fresh basil,
    roughly torn
Salt and freshly ground black pepper

1. Put the flour and cocoa powder into a food processor and process for a few seconds until mixed together. Add the eggs and process until the mixture has formed into rough breadcrumbs.

2. Tip out onto a lightly floured work surface and knead just until the dough is smooth. Divide into four pieces. Start on the widest setting on the pasta machine and feed the dough through the rollers. Dust the strip of dough with flour.

3. Narrow the setting and feed the dough through again. Keep doing this, dusting with flour each time, until you have finished on the narrowest setting. Once you have a long strip of pasta dough, dust with flour and fold four or five times over, then cut into 5mm strips. Repeat for the remaining three pieces of dough.

4. To make the sauce, heat the olive oil in a saucepan and add the garlic and rosemary. Cook for a minute, then pour in the chopped tomatoes and chilli. Season with salt and freshly ground black pepper and add a pinch of sugar. Cook for 30–40 minutes until the sauce is really thick. Just before serving stir in the torn basil leaves.

5. Meanwhile, cook the pasta in a large pan of salted boiling water for 3–4 minutes. Drain and toss with the tomato sauce. Serve fresh grated Parmesan on the side.

INDEX